Basic Business Law: Essential Legal Concepts for Entrepreneurs and Managers

Logan Sharpe

Table of contents

Introduction: Start Smart: Law as Leverage

The modern entrepreneur lives in a paradox: never has it been easier to start a business, yet never has the terrain been more fraught with hidden legal traps. A simple online form can register your company in minutes, but one unchecked clause can sink it just as fast. The digital economy rewards speed and adaptability, but law rewards precision and foresight. Between those two forces—momentum and compliance—stands the entrepreneur, trying to make sense of what truly matters. Most founders, managers, and freelancers operate with a quiet anxiety that at any moment, they might trip over a rule they didn't even know existed. Not because they are careless, but because the law is a foreign language written for another audience. Lawyers spend years learning it; entrepreneurs are expected to improvise in it.

This book was written to close that gap—to translate legal thinking into practical business sense. You don't need to memorize case law or interpret statutes like an attorney. What you need is to think legally enough to make smarter decisions and spot when to call for help. Think of it as defensive driving for business: you can't control the weather, but you can recognize the signs of a storm. Competence, not mastery, is the goal; fluency, not expertise. Knowing just enough to prevent disasters and accelerate what already works.

Entrepreneurs tend to see law as friction—paperwork, contracts, waiting for approvals, paying for opinions. But the truth is that law, when understood as a framework instead of a barrier, becomes leverage. It defines ownership, protects innovation, and builds trust in markets. Every great company, from a small family business to a multinational, stands on a foundation of enforceable promises. Contracts are simply formalized trust; trademarks are brand identity in legal armor; corporate structures are shields against chaos. The law, when used intelligently, amplifies your control over risk and reward.

And yet, most founders admit they only deal with legal issues reactively. They call a lawyer when something goes wrong: a partner walks away, a client refuses payment, a competitor imitates their brand. That reactive posture costs exponentially more than a proactive one. The law punishes ignorance not with fines alone, but with uncertainty. What this book proposes is a shift from fear to fluency—from avoidance to empowerment. You will not become a lawyer by reading it, but you will stop being vulnerable to the things lawyers make money fixing.

The truth is that most legal problems stem from patterns, not surprises. A business contract, for instance, isn't a mystical text; it's a record of expectations. If both parties understand the risks, timelines, and consequences, the document simply reflects clarity. If they don't, no number of clauses can save them. What you will learn in these pages is not just terminology, but mindset: how to see legal relationships as systems that either create value or leak it. A founder who knows what makes a clause dangerous, what makes an agreement enforceable, or what makes a structure tax-efficient is already ahead of 80% of their competitors.

Consider the early days of a startup. Enthusiasm is high, resources are scarce, and the temptation is to "deal with the legal stuff later." But the habits you set in motion on day one—who owns what, who decides what, who gets paid how—shape your destiny. Many promising ventures collapse not because the idea was flawed, but because the relationships were. One partner assumed equal ownership, another assumed sweat equity, and the law, being silent on assumptions, enforces only what is written. Clarity is not bureaucracy; it is survival.

Legal literacy also saves time. The entrepreneur who can read a basic nondisclosure agreement, identify red flags in a service contract, or negotiate a term sheet without freezing, is far more agile in the real world. Lawyers then become allies instead of translators. You can ask sharper questions, reject unnecessary complexity, and understand the difference between "risky" and "unnecessary." You learn when to protect, when to negotiate, and when to walk away. The speed advantage of the legally literate entrepreneur isn't theoretical—it's measurable. Deals close faster, mistakes get caught earlier, and relationships stay cleaner.

The law can seem abstract until it hits your bank account. Taxes, for example, are not just obligations; they are incentives coded into the system. Intellectual property rights are not just protection; they are assets you can license, sell, or collateralize. Employment law isn't just compliance; it's how you build culture without stepping into litigation. When you see law as leverage, you start noticing how every successful company uses it not to slow down, but to structure growth. Apple's trademark portfolio is a fortress; Tesla's open patents are a strategic gesture; small e-commerce sellers use LLCs to separate personal and business liability. These aren't random moves—they're legal design decisions.

But entrepreneurs often tell themselves a story: that law is for big companies, that small ones can fly under the radar. That illusion lasts until a client doesn't pay, an investor asks for due diligence, or a competitor files a complaint. The legal system does not scale by size; it scales by exposure. A freelancer with one client has just as much to lose in relative terms as a corporation. The law doesn't care about your intent—it cares about your documentation. That's why understanding the essentials is not optional, even for the smallest player.

There is also a psychological benefit to competence. When you understand the rules, you make decisions with confidence. Fear shrinks. The "what if" scenarios that once paralyzed you become manageable variables. The anxiety that something invisible could ruin you gives way to strategy. Law stops being a shadow overhead and becomes a tool in your hand. You can navigate conversations with investors, suppliers, and clients with composure. You can read agreements and actually understand what you're committing to. You can sense when someone is bluffing behind legal jargon. This confidence builds credibility—the kind that attracts trust from partners and respect from professionals.

The challenge, of course, is information overload. Legal systems are vast, fragmented, and constantly evolving. No one can know it all. That's why this book focuses on what matters most to your decisions: the minimum effective knowledge. Each chapter isolates a fundamental area—business formation, contracts, employment, intellectual property, finance, and dispute prevention—and distills the principles that drive real-world outcomes. It's not about memorizing articles of law; it's about internalizing patterns of reasoning. Once you grasp those patterns, you can adapt them anywhere, from signing a lease to negotiating a partnership.

You'll learn how to read the architecture of agreements rather than just their words. You'll see how rights and obligations interact like gears, how liability shifts through clauses, and how incentives align or clash. You'll understand why a well-drafted contract is not just protection but communication—an honest record of intent. You'll explore how legal structures affect not just taxes but power dynamics: who controls the company, who bears risk, who reaps reward. Each principle will be grounded in real entrepreneurial context, not textbook abstraction.

At the heart of it all lies a simple truth: law rewards those who respect it early. The earlier you integrate legal thinking into your business model, the less you will pay in corrections later. Preventive law is like preventive medicine—it feels optional until it's not. A founder who spends two hours defining equity terms avoids two years of conflict. A manager who documents performance standards prevents a lawsuit. A brand that registers its trademarks before scaling avoids rebranding under pressure. Every minute invested in legal clarity compounds over time.

This first chapter sets the foundation for that shift—from reactive panic to proactive control. You will learn to see the law not as an obstacle but as a form of structure that gives your business shape. It is the invisible skeleton that allows creativity to move safely. When understood and respected, it doesn't slow you down; it keeps you standing when the storm hits. The following chapters will not drown you in citations but will equip you with frameworks you can actually apply tomorrow morning.

By the end of this journey, you will not think like a lawyer, and that's the point. You will think like an entrepreneur who speaks enough legal to protect what you build. You'll know what questions to ask, when to call for help, and when to trust your own judgment. You'll be capable of seeing legal risk as a design variable, not a threat. The goal isn't perfection—it's resilience.

Competence and confidence: that's the real reward of learning business law as leverage. Because once you stop fearing the landmines, you can finally focus on building the road.

Every business, no matter its size or ambition, stands on a legal architecture—an invisible frame that determines how power, responsibility, and reward are distributed. Before a single product is sold or a single hire is made, a structure already exists, even if it's only implied. The law recognizes that structure, whether you've chosen it or not. That is why we start here—with formation and governance. It's the skeleton of everything that follows. A freelancer, a startup, a family business, or a growing company must all answer the same essential question: *what shape should my business take?* The decision is not purely administrative—it affects your taxes, liability, reputation, and long-term freedom. A sole proprietorship gives simplicity but no shield. A limited liability company offers protection but requires discipline. A corporation creates permanence and access to capital, but at the cost of formalities. Understanding how each works in practice—not just in law—is the first step to thinking strategically rather than reactively.

Once the structure is sound, governance enters the picture. Governance is not a word reserved for large boards and shareholder meetings. It's the set of rules that keep your decisions coherent as you grow. Who decides what, who can sign contracts, who controls the bank account—these are not trivialities; they are the difference between smooth operations and internal chaos. Many partnerships dissolve not because of betrayal, but because there was never a clear decision-making process. A written operating agreement or partnership contract may seem unnecessary when everyone gets along, but it is precisely that clarity that prevents misunderstandings from turning into lawsuits. Good governance, at any scale, is like oxygen: invisible when present, disastrous when absent.

From there, the journey shifts to the tools of daily commerce—the legal language that defines your relationships. Contracts are not enemies; they are maps of expectation. They translate trust into structure. In plain English, they define what each side gives, what each side gets, and what happens when things go wrong. This book will demystify the anatomy of a contract—the clauses that matter, the traps to avoid, and the principles that repeat across industries. You will learn to see contracts not as weapons or shields, but as instruments of clarity. Even a simple service agreement between two parties can teach more about fairness and foresight than a hundred pages of theory. You'll see how each clause—payment terms, termination rights, warranties—reflects a hidden negotiation of risk. By the end, you'll be able to read a contract like a story, tracing motives and consequences rather than drowning in jargon.

But legal fluency doesn't stop with contracts. It extends into every touchpoint of modern business—your brand, your customers, your people. Marketing and intellectual property, for example, are now inseparable. Every slogan, logo, and campaign carries legal implications. A name you fall in love with might already belong to someone else. A photograph you find online may cost you thousands in infringement claims. A privacy disclaimer you skip can expose you to regulators. Yet, behind every compliance rule lies an opportunity to differentiate yourself through transparency and professionalism. Consumers trust companies that handle data responsibly, that protect customer rights, and that communicate clearly. Intellectual property, far from being an abstract legal category, becomes the language of identity. Whether it's a trademark protecting your name or a copyright protecting your content, understanding how ownership works allows creativity to thrive without fear.

Then comes the human element: employment. Managing people is as much a legal act as it is a moral one. Hiring, training, firing, and contracting all involve rights and duties that shape your culture. Each decision—whether to use employees or contractors, how to document expectations, how to handle disputes—has legal ripples. You'll see how labor laws, when respected early, prevent resentment and instability later. A good employment contract, like any solid agreement, protects both sides and establishes mutual clarity. It's not about suspicion; it's about structure.

The next stage is money—the bloodstream of every venture. Here law meets finance, and both demand precision. Fundraising, for instance, is not merely convincing investors to believe in you; it's about defining what they own and what they control. A miswritten investment agreement can hand away more power than you realize. Equity, debt, convertible notes, crowdfunding—all have legal identities that dictate your future flexibility. You'll learn to navigate these terms without needing to be a financial engineer. Understanding the core logic behind each instrument helps you negotiate confidently and recognize fair terms before signing anything.

Finally, the road leads to risk: disputes, liabilities, and the art of prevention. Every disagreement is a test of how well your foundation was built. When the paperwork is clear, and expectations were aligned, disputes shrink to manageable proportions. When everything was verbal, emotional, or improvised, they explode. This book will help you think defensively without becoming paranoid. You'll learn how to document decisions, how to store evidence, how to communicate under potential conflict, and how to know when silence is safer than speech. The goal is not to live in fear of being sued—it's to make litigation unnecessary by structuring your relationships so that trust and recourse coexist.

Each chapter in this book follows this arc—from foundation to tools to money and risk—because that is the natural rhythm of entrepreneurship itself. Businesses grow like trees: they need roots before branches, structure before movement. The foundation chapters teach you to choose wisely and build consciously. The daily tools chapters show you how to operate with integrity and foresight. The money and risk chapters train you to sustain growth without imploding under pressure. None of this is theory for theory's sake. Every concept comes with examples from real cases—some drawn from major corporations, others from small entrepreneurs who learned lessons the hard way. You'll see what happens when founders ignore structure, when marketers misuse intellectual property, or when investors misunderstand terms. The lessons are practical because they are lived.

Most importantly, this book is written in plain language. You will not find paragraphs full of citations or academic digressions. The purpose here is utility, not decoration. Legal understanding should feel accessible, even empowering. Every section includes ideas that can be applied immediately: how to test a contract's fairness, how to draft basic terms, how to structure ownership discussions, how to respond to a client who refuses payment. The goal is not to overwhelm you with law, but to help you recognize patterns—the recurring ways in which rights, duties, and risks appear in business life. Once you see the pattern, you can predict and prevent problems long before they surface.

When you finish this journey, you will have something far more valuable than memorized rules: intuition. You will sense when a deal feels off, when a clause hides imbalance, when a partner's proposal masks risk. You will learn how to flag early warning signs and translate them into decisive, informed action. That is the essence of leverage—not the avoidance of risk, but the intelligent management of it.

The path through this book is designed to be progressive. Each chapter builds upon the last, layering knowledge the way a builder lays bricks—one row securing the next. Skipping ahead might feel tempting, especially if you have an urgent problem in contracts or employment, but resist the impulse. The logic of law mirrors the logic of business: without structure, tools lose purpose; without governance, agreements collapse. Reading in sequence ensures that your understanding matures organically. You'll learn not just *what* to do, but *why* it matters. The early chapters establish context—why structure shapes liability, how ownership defines authority, how written clarity prevents future chaos. The later chapters turn that understanding into precision—

how to apply contracts, how to protect creativity, how to handle conflict and money flow.

At every stage, remember that law is not absolute; it's local. Jurisdictions differ widely, and what's permitted in one country—or even one state—might be restricted in another. Employment laws, privacy regulations, tax codes, and intellectual property rules shift with geography. The examples here are based on common frameworks and best practices derived from multiple legal systems, but they cannot replace professional counsel. The aim is to make you competent enough to recognize when expertise is required. Think of this book as a map, not a verdict. It helps you navigate unfamiliar territory, but when the terrain gets tricky, you still need a guide who knows the local ground.

Flagging "triggers" is a habit every businessperson should cultivate. These are moments when the complexity or risk level jumps—when you're about to sign a long-term lease, issue shares, expand internationally, fire an employee, or collect customer data. Recognizing those triggers early allows you to bring in legal help strategically, not reactively. You'll also learn how to brief a lawyer efficiently, which saves time and money. The most expensive hours in legal work are spent on clarification—when the client doesn't know what they want or fails to provide organized information. The checklists in this book are designed to eliminate that waste. They help you prepare the right documents, ask the right questions, and communicate your objectives clearly. A well-prepared entrepreneur can cut legal costs in half simply by being specific.

This approach fosters a healthier relationship with the legal system itself. Instead of seeing lawyers as firefighters called only when something burns, you start seeing them as engineers who help you reinforce the structure before it cracks. Preventive law may not feel urgent, but it's the quiet backbone of every stable company. When you know what to look for, legal counsel becomes a precision tool rather than a blunt instrument.

As you move forward, keep in mind that the examples, cases, and models in this book are drawn from real practice but generalized to fit a wide audience. They represent principles, not prescriptions. The reality of your business—its scale, jurisdiction, and culture—will always introduce nuances that demand customization. What remains universal is the mindset: seek clarity, respect structure, and never postpone documentation. Law punishes vagueness and rewards precision. Every paragraph ahead is written to help you think like someone who understands that truth.

And so, we begin at the origin point—the moment where ideas meet form. Before profits, before teams, before branding, there must be a structure. The right legal foundation doesn't just protect you from loss; it unlocks growth. It defines ownership, credibility, and continuity. Choosing wisely at this stage is not about bureaucracy—it's about freedom. A well-structured business can pivot, expand, attract investors, and survive crises without losing its integrity. The next chapter will guide you through that first and most consequential decision: how to choose a structure that protects your work and gives your ambition room to grow.

Chapter 1 — Choose Structure and Governance

Every business begins with a decision that is at once simple and profound: what form will it take? To outsiders, this question might sound administrative, almost bureaucratic, but entrepreneurs who have lived through a dispute or an audit know better. The choice of entity is the legal DNA of a business—it determines how you're taxed, who bears the risk, and how money, control, and responsibility circulate. It's the difference between sleeping well and waking up to a lawsuit that reaches into your personal savings. It's the line separating a dream that scales from one that collapses under paperwork or investor hesitation. Structure, in other words, is not just about paperwork; it's about power, protection, and potential.

The starting point for most small ventures is the **sole proprietorship**, a deceptively simple form. It appeals to those who want to move fast: no formal registration, minimal accounting, total control. For freelancers, artisans, and early-stage entrepreneurs testing an idea, it feels liberating. But that freedom comes at a price—the entrepreneur *is* the business. There is no legal separation. If a client sues, if a supplier goes unpaid, if an accident happens, personal assets are on the line. Your car, your home, your bank account can all become part of the fallout. The tax side is equally intertwined: profits are reported as personal income, which means simplicity but no flexibility. While that can be fine for small-scale operations, it limits growth. Banks hesitate to lend, investors have no shares to buy, and transferring ownership becomes a legal maze. A sole proprietorship is fast to start but fragile to sustain.

Next comes the **partnership**, which might look like the natural evolution—two or more people joining forces. Partnerships come in flavors: general partnerships, limited partnerships, and variations shaped by national law. What binds them is shared profit and shared exposure. A general partnership, unless otherwise defined, means each partner can bind the business and is personally liable for its debts. The law assumes mutual agency; if your partner signs a deal, you are on the hook even if you never saw the paper. Many friendships and family ventures have ended in silence because of this legal truth. A limited partnership, by contrast, separates control from contribution—one or more partners manage, others invest but remain shielded from liability. This structure can work when capital and talent come from different people. Yet, the partnership form, while intimate and flexible, depends entirely on trust and clarity. Without a written agreement spelling out roles, capital contributions, exit rules, and decision rights, what begins as collaboration often becomes conflict. The law's default assumptions rarely match real intentions.

As businesses mature, most entrepreneurs seek protection—an entity that separates personal and corporate life. Enter the **limited liability company**, often called an LLC. It is the modern entrepreneur's favorite invention: simple to form, adaptable, and protective. The key advantage lies in the name—*limited liability*. The company is a separate legal person; it owns its assets, carries its debts, and faces its lawsuits. In principle, your personal property stays safe. That principle, however, holds only if you respect the boundary. Commingling personal and business funds, failing to maintain basic records, or using the company as a personal bank account can "pierce the veil," reuniting you with liability. The LLC blends flexibility with formality—you can structure it like a partnership or like a corporation, choose how it's taxed, and distribute profits almost any way you like. For most startups, consultancies, and small enterprises, it strikes the best balance between simplicity and safety.

The **corporation**, by contrast, is the oldest and most structured of the forms. It's the fortress of business law: rigid in rules but powerful in scale. A corporation exists independently of its owners, governed by a board of directors and officers who make decisions on behalf of shareholders. That separation creates permanence—ownership can change hands without affecting operations. It's also what investors love. Venture capitalists, angel funds, and institutional players prefer corporations because shares, bylaws, and governance frameworks are predictable. They know where their money goes and what rights it buys. The tax picture, however, is more complex. In many systems, corporations face "double taxation": profits are taxed at the corporate level, and dividends again at the personal level. Some jurisdictions mitigate this with pass-through options or reduced rates, but it remains a factor. The administrative burden—meetings, minutes, resolutions—is also heavier. Yet for those aiming to raise significant capital or go public, incorporation is the unavoidable route.

Choosing among these forms isn't about prestige; it's about fit. The right structure depends on how you plan to grow, how you manage risk, and what kind of relationships you expect with partners and investors. Many founders, seduced by the speed of a sole proprietorship or partnership, postpone formalization until it's too late. They discover, during their first serious negotiation, that they can't issue equity, can't sign efficiently, or can't prove who owns what. Investors look at that confusion and walk away. No matter how innovative your product, if your ownership records are messy, your company becomes uninvestable. The same goes for taxes: a structure chosen without foresight can drain profits through unnecessary liabilities. Moving from one entity to another is possible but costly; the earlier you make the right choice, the stronger your foundation.

Beyond the technicalities of tax and liability lies something subtler but no less vital—**alignment among founders**. The structure you choose is only as stable as the relationships it houses. Founders often avoid difficult conversations in the beginning, fearing they'll dampen enthusiasm. Yet, unspoken assumptions about ownership, time commitment, or future roles are legal time bombs. Governance begins the moment two people agree to build something together. If one imagines equal shares and the other expects a merit-based distribution, friction is inevitable. If one sees the company as a short-term project and the other as a lifelong mission, decisions will diverge. Formalizing expectations through documents—operating agreements, shareholder pacts, vesting schedules—is not an act of distrust; it's an act of maturity. It forces clarity before emotions blur the lines.

Governance also scales with ambition. In small teams, governance may mean monthly meetings and transparent finances. In larger organizations, it evolves into a full ecosystem—boards, committees, audits. But the principle remains the same: authority must match accountability. A clear chain of decision-making prevents paralysis and politics. Without it, even the best structure becomes hollow. Investors, in particular, examine governance as closely as they examine financials. They want to know that decisions aren't arbitrary, that conflicts of interest are managed, and that the founders have systems for resolving disagreements. Good governance signals seriousness.

From a tax perspective, the differences between entities can be dramatic. A sole proprietor or partnership typically faces *pass-through* taxation: profits are treated as personal income, avoiding corporate tax but potentially pushing the owner into higher brackets. An LLC offers flexibility—you can elect to be taxed as a partnership or corporation, depending on what benefits you most. Corporations, while subject to more layers of taxation, gain access to deductions, benefits, and reinvestment structures unavailable to individuals. Each option carries trade-offs. The clever entrepreneur doesn't chase the lowest tax rate blindly; they choose the configuration that aligns with their growth trajectory and risk profile.

The question of fundraising ties it all together. Investors, by nature, seek clarity and enforceable rights. They need to know who owns what, how decisions are made, and how their returns will be structured. A sole proprietorship cannot accommodate investors; partnerships make equity negotiation messy; LLCs can attract smaller investors or private deals; corporations open the door to professional capital. The more formal the structure, the easier it becomes to issue shares, define voting rights, and comply with securities laws. Founders who plan for external funding should think ahead—not because they must raise money tomorrow, but because retrofitting governance later can scare away serious backers.

Clean ownership records are the cornerstone of all this. Every share, every contribution, every transfer must be documented. Many startups discover only when preparing for acquisition or funding that their cap table is chaos—missing agreements, overlapping claims, unsigned documents. That confusion can kill a deal overnight. The legal concept of "title" matters here: if you can't prove ownership, you don't truly own it. That applies not only to equity but to intellectual property. Code written by freelancers, designs created by contractors, even brand names coined by partners must be properly assigned to the company. Without that, investors hesitate, and acquirers flee. Clarity equals credibility.

Structure and governance, then, are not abstract legal categories—they are the architecture of trust. They shape how the world perceives your business and how your team operates within it. They decide whether risk is contained or contagious, whether profits flow efficiently or leak through oversight. Choosing wisely doesn't guarantee success, but choosing poorly almost guarantees regret.

As we move deeper into the book, you'll see how every legal decision—contracts, employment, branding, financing—rests on this foundation. The entity you form today dictates the freedoms and constraints of tomorrow. Take the time to understand it, to align with your co-founders, to record it with precision. A well-built structure doesn't just protect you; it frees you to focus on what truly matters—building something that lasts.

Once the structure is chosen, the next step is giving that structure a soul—a body of documents that make it real, coherent, and functional. Many founders assume that forming a company begins and ends with registration papers. In truth, that's only the birth certificate. What keeps the company alive and legally sound are its internal agreements—the constitution, the operating rules, and the records of ownership. These documents are the grammar of governance: they make sure everyone speaks the same language when making decisions, raising money, or resolving conflict.

At the core lies the **articles of incorporation** or **charter**, depending on jurisdiction. This is the public declaration of your company's existence—the document that turns an idea into a recognized legal entity. It states the company's name, purpose, address, and share structure. To outsiders, it signals legitimacy; to the state, it defines responsibility. For a corporation, it sets out how many shares can exist, their classes, and what powers each class holds. For an LLC, it often simply records existence, leaving internal arrangements for the **operating agreement**. The articles are usually short, but deceptively powerful. A misplaced clause about voting rights or share classes can echo for years. It's the skeleton upon which every later decision hangs.

Then comes the **bylaws** (for corporations) or the **operating agreement** (for LLCs). If the articles are the birth certificate, these are the living rules. They define how decisions are made, who holds authority, how meetings are conducted, how profits are distributed, and how ownership changes hands. Without them, even small issues—like who can open a bank account or sign a lease—can stall progress. For corporations, bylaws often dictate the relationship between shareholders, directors, and officers: when the board must meet, what constitutes a quorum, how votes are counted. In an LLC, the operating agreement is the most flexible document in the entire business world—it can mimic a partnership, a corporation, or something entirely unique. It can define how members contribute capital, how profits are split, how managers are appointed, and how disputes are handled.

The best operating agreements are not written for courts; they're written for clarity. They prevent small misunderstandings from metastasizing into existential threats. Many founders discover their agreement is missing only when a partner departs or demands a payout. Having one in place from the beginning does not slow you down—it saves you from paralysis later.

Equally vital is the **founder equity and vesting structure**. At the start of a company, ownership is cheap. Shares feel symbolic, not real. But as value grows, those symbols turn into leverage, control, and potential fortune. Without a vesting plan—an agreement that founders "earn" their equity over time—early enthusiasm can become a trap. Imagine a co-founder leaving six months in, yet retaining half the company. That dead equity will haunt every negotiation with future investors or hires. Vesting solves this by aligning ownership with commitment. It typically unfolds over years, releasing shares gradually as milestones are met. It's a way of saying: we all share the reward when we all share the work.

Related to this is **cap table hygiene**, a phrase that sounds technical but simply means keeping an accurate, up-to-date record of who owns what. The capitalization table, or cap table, lists every shareholder, the number of shares, their class, and any options or warrants outstanding. It evolves with every investment, grant, or transfer. When maintained properly, it becomes a mirror of your company's structure—clear, credible, and ready for scrutiny. When neglected, it becomes a swamp of confusion that scares investors and lawyers alike. Cap table mistakes—unrecorded transfers, overlapping claims, missing signatures—are not minor; they are time bombs. Cleaning them later can take months and cost tens of thousands in legal fees. Maintaining it correctly from the start is a discipline that signals professionalism and integrity.

The next layer of governance is behavioral rather than structural: **maintaining the liability shield**. Having a company doesn't automatically protect you if your behavior contradicts it. The law respects formality—it distinguishes between personal and corporate actions. To preserve that separation, you must live it daily. First, keep finances distinct. Business accounts must remain separate from personal ones; mixing funds can pierce the corporate veil and expose you personally. Pay yourself formally, record expenses properly, and keep documentation for every transfer. Second, respect decision-making procedures. Major actions—signing contracts, taking loans, issuing shares—should be authorized by the proper body, whether that's the members of an LLC or the board of a corporation. Document those approvals in **minutes** or **written consents**. Even a single-page note summarizing a meeting's decisions, dated and signed, can make the difference between order and chaos in a dispute.

Authority to sign is another underestimated cornerstone. In early stages, everyone feels empowered to make commitments, but in law, only those explicitly authorized can bind the company. A rogue signature can lead to enforceable obligations the rest of the team never approved. Establishing who can sign—what, when, and up to what limit—keeps your risk contained. This doesn't have to mean bureaucracy. A clear policy, even an internal memo, can suffice as long as it's consistent and respected.

Finally, **governance cadence**—the rhythm of decision-making—keeps everything fluid. Entrepreneurs often equate meetings with wasted time, but the right cadence transforms them into a control mechanism. A monthly or quarterly review of finances, strategy, and compliance is enough to stay aligned and legally sound. It ensures that when the board or members sign off on major moves, they do so knowingly. This rhythm also produces documentation—minutes, consents, updates—that prove diligence. In the eyes of investors, regulators, or courts, those records show responsibility. And responsibility, in business law, is the twin of credibility.

Good governance, therefore, isn't about paperwork for its own sake—it's about protection, memory, and speed. It ensures that when someone asks, "Who decided this?" you can answer without hesitation. That clarity keeps operations agile because trust in the process eliminates hesitation. A founder confident in their documentation can move decisively, secure in the knowledge that authority and accountability are clear. The paradox is that structure—when done right—doesn't slow you down. It's the very thing that allows you to move faster without fear of collapse.

To see how structure and governance operate in real life, it helps to look through the eyes of two very different founders. The first is a solo consultant named Maria, launching a professional services business offering marketing strategy to small firms. The second is a pair of founders—James and Priya—developing a tech startup they hope will attract venture capital within a year. Both are entrepreneurs, both have ambition, but their legal needs diverge sharply.

Maria's decision rests on flexibility and simplicity. Her clients pay directly for her time and expertise. She has no employees, no investors, and minimal risk beyond professional liability. The **LLC** becomes her natural ally. It shields her personal assets, allows her to elect pass-through taxation so profits appear directly on her tax return, and requires limited formalities. She opens a dedicated business account, drafts an operating agreement even though she's the sole member, and keeps concise records of her income and expenses. Her governance cadence is light—quarterly reviews, annual filings, and careful separation of funds. She doesn't need a board or stock certificates; she needs clarity. The LLC lets her appear credible to clients and banks without drowning in paperwork.

The main advantage for Maria is taxation and protection. Pass-through treatment means she avoids corporate tax altogether—her profits are taxed once as personal income. But this also means she must plan for that tax personally, setting aside reserves and tracking deductible expenses. The trade-off is worth it because it keeps her administrative load small. Investors are irrelevant in her model; she values autonomy. Her legal system mirrors her business philosophy: lean, personal, and transparent. The LLC gives her all the liability protection she needs without creating a complex bureaucracy.

Now contrast that with James and Priya's situation. They're building a software platform and already pitching to venture capital firms. Their investors expect a **C corporation**—in the U.S., typically a Delaware corporation—because it's standardized, predictable, and compatible with preferred stock structures. Venture funds rarely invest in LLCs because of tax complications and uncertainty about ownership transfers. By choosing a corporation early, the founders align with investor expectations and avoid a painful conversion later. They file articles of incorporation outlining multiple share classes: common shares for founders, preferred shares for future investors. They adopt bylaws detailing the board's authority, issue founder stock subject to four-year vesting, and maintain a precise cap table. Every issuance is recorded with timestamps and signatures, ensuring no ambiguity in ownership.

For them, the tax picture flips. Their corporation will face double taxation: once at the corporate level, then again on dividends. But in early stages, profits are minimal and reinvested, so the double tax is largely theoretical. The benefits outweigh the costs. The corporate form allows them to grant stock options to employees, to raise capital easily, and to present an image of formality to partners. Investors can see the governance map: who the directors are, how decisions are approved, what rights attach to their shares. This predictability builds trust.

The limits are also clear. Corporate governance demands more discipline. Board meetings, formal resolutions, and record-keeping become routine. Decisions can't be made impulsively, because authority must flow through proper channels. Yet, those same procedures create legitimacy. When the startup later faces due diligence for funding, their clean paperwork—articles, bylaws, stock issuances, and minutes—will save weeks of stress. The difference between "we think we did that" and "here's the signed record" can determine whether funding closes or collapses.

These two examples—Maria's LLC and the tech team's corporation—illustrate the central truth: there is no universal best entity. There are only trade-offs. An LLC offers flexibility, but venture investors avoid it. A corporation attracts capital, but adds complexity. Pass-through taxation simplifies early life, but limits reinvestment. Corporate taxation adds friction, but supports scalability. What matters is alignment—choosing the structure that fits your goals and risk tolerance, not someone else's.

Once the entity is formed, maintenance becomes the silent discipline. Annual filings, tax returns, registered agents, and periodic reviews are the heartbeat of compliance. Ignoring them is like skipping oil changes in a new car—it runs fine until it doesn't. Entrepreneurs who view these rituals as part of their business rhythm rarely face crises. Those who neglect them often learn the hard way that the law forgets nothing.

A practical mental checklist emerges: the company is formed; the ownership is documented; authority is clear; finances are separated; decisions are recorded; taxes are filed. That's the foundation of good governance. It might sound mundane, but it's the invisible structure that lets ambition breathe safely. Investors, partners, and clients don't expect perfection—they expect order.

With the house now framed—structure chosen, documents in place, governance alive—the business can begin to move. The next step is understanding the legal tissue that holds it together day by day: the contracts. Every promise, every sale, every hire lives or dies by them. The coming chapter will translate those agreements from legalese into leverage, showing how a well-written contract becomes not a shield against conflict, but a roadmap to trust.

Chapter 2 — Contracts that Protect You

Every business relationship begins with a promise. A promise to deliver, to pay, to perform. In the earliest days of commerce, a handshake sealed that promise, backed by reputation and trust. But as transactions grew more complex—spanning borders, involving third parties, blending services and technology—trust alone became fragile currency. Today, a written contract is not a sign of distrust; it's the architecture of cooperation. It gives shape to intention, transforming goodwill into something measurable and enforceable. Entrepreneurs who rely on verbal understandings discover, often painfully, that memory fades faster than obligation. Handshakes may start friendships, but they rarely survive disputes.

A contract, at its essence, is not mystical. It's a structured record of mutual understanding. The law recognizes it when certain ingredients are present: an offer, an acceptance, and consideration. These three words—so often buried in legal textbooks—form the foundation of nearly every commercial relationship.

An **offer** is the clear expression of willingness to enter into an agreement on defined terms. It must show intent to be bound once accepted. A proposal like "I might sell you my equipment next month if I feel like it" isn't an offer; it's an idea. An offer says, "I will sell you this equipment for €10,000, delivery next week." The clarity transforms casual talk into commitment.

Acceptance is the mirror image of that offer—a clear, unqualified agreement to its terms. When the buyer says, "I agree,

I'll pay €10,000 for delivery next week," the contract crystallizes. If instead the buyer replies, "I'll take it for €9,000," that's not acceptance—it's a counteroffer. The beauty of this structure is that it ensures both sides truly meet in the middle. There's no ambiguity about what was promised or expected.

Then comes **consideration**, the concept that breathes life into the promise. It's the exchange of value—money, services, goods, effort, or even a promise to refrain from doing something. Without consideration, a contract is a gift, not a bargain, and the law doesn't enforce gifts in business. Consideration is the "why" behind the deal, the proof that each party is giving something up to gain something else. It doesn't need to be equal in value—only real and mutual.

Once those three elements align, a contract exists. But existence and enforceability are two different things. For a contract to hold in court, it must also meet several secondary tests: capacity, legality, consent, and certainty. Each one sounds obvious until it's not.

Capacity means that the people entering the agreement have the legal ability to do so. Minors, individuals of unsound mind, or companies lacking proper authority can't bind themselves validly. In business, this often appears in subtle form—a manager signs a contract beyond their delegated authority, or a new company executes an agreement before it legally exists. The result is an unenforceable promise that creates more confusion than protection. That's why establishing **authority to sign** is critical. Every company should know who has the right to bind it and within what limits. A careless signature can turn enthusiasm into liability.

Legality seems self-evident, but history is littered with deals voided because their purpose violated regulation or public policy. A marketing agency that promises "guaranteed Google rankings" through manipulative methods, a consultancy contracting in areas requiring unlicensed practice, a company agreeing to sell goods that breach import laws—all these contracts fail at the root. The law will not enforce what the law forbids.

Consent is another quiet fault line. For a contract to stand, it must be entered freely, without fraud, duress, or undue influence. In the business context, this often surfaces in rushed deals, misleading statements, or power imbalances. A small vendor pressured into signing a one-sided contract with a multinational might later claim coercion. Courts examine not only what was written, but how it was agreed. Transparency, negotiation, and the absence of trickery protect both sides from later claims of invalid consent.

Certainty, finally, demands that the contract's terms are clear enough to enforce. Vague promises—"deliver a reasonable amount," "provide satisfactory services"—sound flexible but invite dispute. What's "reasonable" to one side is "unfair" to the other. The clearer the wording, the stronger the protection. A good contract is specific enough to leave no room for creative memory.

Even with those principles understood, entrepreneurs often stumble on the mechanics—how a contract is executed and what makes a signature binding. In the digital age, this has become more relevant than ever. Does an email count? What about an electronic signature? The answer depends on intent and evidence. The key is not the ink but the intention to be bound and the ability to verify authenticity. A scanned signature, a DocuSign confirmation, or a simple email exchange saying "I agree to these terms" can all form enforceable contracts if they show clear mutual consent. Courts increasingly recognize that commerce flows digitally, and the law has evolved to follow.

Authority remains a cornerstone. Within a company, not everyone who uses its letterhead has the power to make promises on its behalf. A sales representative might negotiate but not sign. A project manager may approve expenses but not contractual obligations. When a dispute arises, one of the first questions asked is: *Was this person authorized?* The answer determines whether the company or the individual bears the consequences. Clear delegation—through internal policy, bylaws, or written resolutions—prevents expensive confusion.

Entrepreneurs sometimes overlook how fragile their liability protection becomes when they act outside their entity's authority. Signing a contract personally, or mixing personal and business signatures, can pierce the corporate veil. Always sign in the name of the entity, with your title beneath: *"ABC Ltd., by Maria Rossi, Managing Director."* That simple line preserves the separation between you and the company.

The enforceability of a contract also depends on what's inside it—the terms themselves. The law doesn't demand perfection, but it does require fairness and mutual understanding. Clauses that are unconscionable—so one-sided they shock reason—can be struck down. Hidden fees, automatic renewals, or penalty clauses that bear no relation to real loss may backfire. A contract must balance risk, not weaponize it. The strongest agreements are those both parties could sign again tomorrow without resentment.

Disputes, when they arise, almost always hide in the gray zones between words. Ambiguity is the enemy of peace. Entrepreneurs often reuse templates found online, assuming one-size-fits-all. They rarely do. A clause copied from a U.S. template might contradict European consumer law; a borrowed confidentiality agreement might omit jurisdiction or remedies. Small omissions—dates, definitions, governing law—become cracks through which conflict seeps.

Common pressure points recur across industries. Payment terms are one: what constitutes delivery, when payment is due, what happens if it's late. Another is scope—what exactly is being provided. Without clarity, clients expect more, providers deliver less, and both feel wronged. Termination clauses, too, generate tension: can the contract be ended early, and if so, under what conditions? Is notice required? Must reasons be given? Every contract should answer these questions explicitly.

Disputes also thrive where communication fails. A signed document is only as strong as the understanding behind it. Parties who rush through negotiation to "just get it signed" often sow the seeds of future resentment. The law enforces what is written, not what was imagined. That's why contracts should be seen as conversations, not chores. Each clause exists because at some point, someone faced that exact problem. Reading them as stories of past conflict gives you foresight into your own.

An overlooked truth about contracts is that they're living tools. They're meant to be referenced, updated, and improved, not stored away. A service agreement written at the birth of a business might fail to reflect its later reality. As operations evolve—new products, new partners, new markets—contracts must evolve too. Keeping them current isn't bureaucracy; it's maintenance, like oiling the hinges of a door that keeps opportunity open.

Good contracts also embody psychology. They manage expectation as much as obligation. The process of drafting forces clarity on both sides. When you write down responsibilities, you discover assumptions you didn't know you had. That moment of discovery is the real value. A written contract is not merely insurance against failure; it's the blueprint for success, defining what success even means.

In the background of all this lies a philosophical shift. Contracts aren't designed to create distance; they create stability. They allow trust to scale beyond personal familiarity. You can't know every supplier, every client, every investor intimately, but you can rely on shared rules. The contract is that shared language. It replaces the uncertainty of personal interpretation with the reliability of written intention.

Understanding where disputes hide—vagueness, authority gaps, ambiguous signatures, unrealistic clauses—is half the battle. The other half is cultural. Build a habit of documenting commitments clearly, even for minor agreements. Send confirmation emails after calls, recap discussions, define deliverables before payment. Those small gestures form the thread that ties business relationships together.

At its highest level, contract literacy is not about drafting from scratch or spotting tricks; it's about alignment. When both sides know exactly what they've agreed to, the relationship runs smoother, and the law remains in the background where it belongs. A good contract doesn't prevent every problem, but it prevents surprise—and in business, surprise is the costliest enemy.

As we move forward, we'll turn from formation to substance—what goes inside the contract and how to read it like a map of risk and responsibility. But first, remember the essential lesson: trust is not diminished by writing; it's refined by it. The handshake may start the story, but the contract ensures it has a fair ending.

Once you understand how contracts are formed, the next step is to master their anatomy. Every contract—no matter how thick or thin, domestic or international—contains a recurring rhythm of clauses that determine where risk lives and who carries it. The words may change, but the structure rarely does. Knowing how to read, negotiate, and reuse these clauses is like learning the grammar of business law. Once fluent, you stop feeling intimidated by length or complexity; you begin to see patterns, predict outcomes, and move faster.

The first and arguably most important clause is **scope and deliverables**. This is the beating heart of every agreement—the section that defines *what* is being done, *how*, *for whom*, and *by when*. Most disputes start here because what was "obvious" to one party wasn't obvious to the other. A vague phrase like "marketing services" can mean anything from a few consulting hours to a full campaign with metrics and creative rights. Clarity here prevents chaos later. A strong scope clause breaks down the deliverables, timelines, and standards of performance without drowning in detail. It should answer the basic test: if someone outside the deal read it, could they understand what success looks like? The key is balance—specific enough to guide, flexible enough to allow adjustment.

The next vital clause deals with **payment and acceptance**. Money terms are the pressure points of every deal. Entrepreneurs often focus on price but overlook timing, milestones, and conditions. When is payment due—upon invoice, delivery, or client approval? What happens if the client delays feedback or refuses acceptance? A well-written payment clause ties deadlines to objective events, not to vague satisfaction. "Payment due thirty days after delivery" is clearer than "after approval," which can be endlessly postponed. Acceptance procedures, too, protect both sides. They define how and when deliverables are deemed complete. Silence after a set period can mean acceptance by default, preventing endless limbo. These details turn cash flow from a guessing game into a predictable rhythm.

Intellectual property clauses—**IP ownership**—are the next battlefield. In the knowledge economy, what you create is often more valuable than what you deliver. Failing to define who owns what can destroy future value. Generally, clients expect to own the final output, but creators must protect their underlying tools, methods, or code. The safest pattern is this: the client owns the deliverable, the vendor retains ownership of pre-existing materials, and both grant each other the licenses necessary to operate. For startups or agencies, this distinction is survival. Without it, you may find yourself unable to reuse your own templates, frameworks, or software libraries because they technically belong to a past client. The law defaults to whoever created the work unless the contract says otherwise—so never leave it unsaid.

Then comes **confidentiality**. It may seem boilerplate, but it's a lifeline for trust. Confidentiality clauses define what information must be protected, how long that protection lasts, and what exceptions apply. They prevent sensitive details—pricing, client lists, trade secrets—from leaking or being reused. Yet, they must also be realistic. Not all information can stay secret forever. Defining "confidential information" narrowly, and including exceptions for public or independently developed data, keeps the clause fair. For early-stage entrepreneurs or consultants, using a standard **NDA**—non-disclosure agreement—before sharing proprietary details is a habit worth cementing. It signals professionalism and safeguards what often matters most: your know-how.

Next are **representations and warranties**, the clauses where each party declares what it knows to be true. The vendor might warrant that their product works as described and doesn't infringe on others' rights; the client might represent that they have the authority and funds to engage. These statements sound ceremonial, but they become the foundation of liability. If a representation proves false, the injured party may have grounds for damages. The trick is to be honest but measured—limit warranties to what you can actually control. Avoid open-ended promises like "our software will perform flawlessly at all times." Instead, use language tied to reasonable standards—"in accordance with specifications" or "as materially described." Overpromising in this section is how optimism becomes exposure.

Indemnities are where real risk lives. To indemnify means to compensate another for loss or harm. In contracts, it's how parties decide who pays if something goes wrong. A client may demand that a vendor indemnify them against lawsuits arising from the vendor's work. The vendor, in turn, might seek reciprocal protection if the client provides defective materials or instructions. The goal isn't to refuse indemnities—they're often unavoidable—but to contain them. Limit them to the areas you actually control (like your own negligence or IP). Broad indemnities that cover "any and all claims of any nature" can bankrupt small businesses. Balance is the keyword: allocate responsibility, don't absorb it all.

Closely tied to indemnities are **limits of liability**—the ceiling on how much one party can owe the other. This clause keeps risk proportionate to reward. A typical formula limits liability to the amount paid under the contract or a multiple of it. Without this cap, even a minor dispute can spiral into existential threat. Exceptions usually exist for intentional misconduct or confidentiality breaches, but for everything else, the limit keeps everyone rational. When you negotiate, don't view this clause as greed or mistrust; it's simply mathematics—no small vendor can shoulder infinite risk for a finite fee.

Termination clauses define how the relationship can end. Every contract should have a beginning, a middle, and a clean exit. Termination for cause—such as breach or non-performance—is standard, but termination for convenience can be a double-edged sword. Clients like flexibility to exit; vendors need predictability. Compromise lies in notice periods and fair compensation for work done. Good termination language prevents emotional blow-ups by making parting procedural, not personal.

Finally, there's **dispute resolution**—the safety valve. It answers the question: when all else fails, where and how will we fight?

You can choose litigation, arbitration, or mediation, and you can decide the jurisdiction and law that govern. This single clause often determines cost and control. Arbitration, for example, is faster and private, but less appealable. Litigation is public but follows stricter evidence rules. Many companies choose mediation first—a non-binding discussion before battle begins. Entrepreneurs often overlook this choice until it's too late, then discover they must defend themselves in a foreign court under unfamiliar law. Always read this clause carefully; it tells you where you'll stand when trust collapses.

When you combine all these clauses, you create what can be called a **contract stack**—a modular toolkit for recurring business relationships. At the base sits the **NDA**, establishing trust before any sensitive conversation. Above that, the **MSA** (Master Service Agreement) sets general terms for long-term collaboration—governing payment, liability, confidentiality, and intellectual property. Then come **SOWs** (Statements of Work), which define each specific project's scope and deliverables. At the top sits the **ToS** (Terms of Service) or similar documents used for customers at scale. Together, this stack saves enormous time and legal expense. Once you've built templates that are fair, defensible, and clear, you can reuse them safely, adjusting details instead of reinventing the wheel.

Negotiation, too, becomes less intimidating when you see it as trading risk, not goodwill. Every clause has weight; shifting one affects others. If a client refuses your liability cap, you might tighten indemnity scope. If they want broader warranties, you can ask for higher payment. The best negotiators don't fight—they rebalance. They speak in principles: "We can agree to that term if we adjust X to keep risk proportional." This shows professionalism and earns respect.

Above all, negotiation should never feel like surrender. You can concede a clause without losing value if you understand its real cost. Many founders panic at redlined documents, assuming lawyers' edits are immovable. In reality, most lawyers expect give and take. The difference between a good and bad negotiation is not who "wins" but who leaves protected enough to keep working together. Contracts are not about dominance—they're about durability.

Theory becomes real when you see it in motion. Take two versions of a service agreement—one written by a vendor, one by a client. Both describe the same project: building a company website. On paper, they look similar—deadlines, payment, deliverables—but the tone and risk allocation are worlds apart.

In the **vendor-friendly** version, payment is front-loaded: fifty percent on signing, fifty percent on delivery. The scope defines what's included and, crucially, what's not. Revisions are limited, and delays caused by the client extend deadlines automatically. Intellectual property transfers only after full payment, ensuring leverage if invoices go unpaid. The limitation of liability caps exposure to the total contract value, and termination for convenience requires thirty days' notice plus payment for all work completed. Dispute resolution favors arbitration in the vendor's home jurisdiction. It's tight, clear, and predictable—the vendor controls the timeline, the risk, and the outcome.

Now flip the script to a **customer-friendly** version. Payment happens only after final approval; acceptance criteria are subjective—"satisfactory to client's standards." The scope includes open-ended "reasonable revisions," and deadlines are fixed regardless of client response times. The vendor must assign all IP upon creation, even before payment clears. The limitation of liability clause disappears entirely, replaced by broad indemnities covering "all losses." Termination for convenience can happen anytime without penalty. Disputes must be litigated in the client's local courts. To the untrained eye, it still looks professional. To the experienced one, it's a minefield. The vendor bears all the risk with little protection.

Most contracts fall somewhere between these extremes, shaped by bargaining power. The more leverage you have—because of expertise, demand, or reputation—the more you can tilt terms in your favor. The goal isn't domination, though; it's sustainability. A good contract allows both sides to profit and trust each other. Contracts that squeeze one side too hard rarely last.

Certain traps, however, appear across all industries. **Auto-renewal** clauses are among the most common. Hidden in small print, they can silently extend contracts for months or years unless canceled within a narrow window. Vendors may use them to secure recurring revenue; clients often discover them too late. The solution is awareness—require written notice before renewal and mark renewal dates in your calendar.

Another recurring trap is **exclusivity**. On paper, exclusivity sounds flattering—a client grants you sole rights to serve them in a certain area or industry. In practice, it can strangle your freedom. Unless compensated properly, exclusivity locks you out of other opportunities. It should always have limits: territory, duration, and purpose. Mutual exclusivity—where both sides limit themselves equally—is rare but fairer.

Most Favored Nation (MFN) clauses are subtler. They promise one party that they'll always receive the best terms you offer anyone else. In isolation, that seems harmless. In reality, it creates administrative chaos and constrains future deals. Imagine giving a discount to a new client; under an MFN, you must retroactively offer it to all others. The clause quietly controls your pricing strategy. If you see "most favored" anything, pause and calculate the hidden cost.

Contracts also bend under **jurisdictional quirks**. In Europe, consumer protection laws can override contract terms, even between businesses if one is small enough. In some U.S. states, non-compete clauses are unenforceable; in others, they're standard. Certain jurisdictions require written notice before termination regardless of what the contract says. These aren't loopholes—they're local realities. Always check governing law clauses against where you actually operate. A beautifully drafted contract governed by foreign law may be worthless if you can't afford to litigate there.

Consumer rules deserve special mention. As more businesses sell directly to individuals online, traditional B2B contracts blend into consumer agreements. Terms of Service (ToS) and Privacy Policies must comply with consumer rights—refunds, data protection, cancellation windows. The same clause that's valid between two companies might be illegal with a private consumer. If your business straddles both worlds, maintain separate versions—one commercial, one consumer-facing.

Before signing any agreement—whether as vendor or client—pause and apply a mental **red flag checklist**. Are the payment terms realistic? Are deliverables clearly defined? Does the contract specify governing law and dispute venue? Are indemnities limited to your own actions? Is there a liability cap? Are renewals and terminations clear? You don't need to be a lawyer to notice imbalance; you need to read slowly and ask questions. If something feels off, it usually is.

Learning to identify these traps changes your posture from defensive to confident. You stop fearing contracts and start using them as tools to shape relationships. You can explain to a client, calmly and professionally, why certain terms need adjustment—not to protect yourself, but to protect the partnership. That's the tone of seasoned entrepreneurs: not combative, but clear.

In practice, the art of contracting is the art of seeing consequences before they happen. Each clause is a lens showing how the relationship might fail—and how to prevent it. Once you learn to read through that lens, you stop signing blindly. You start designing your agreements as carefully as your products or services.

With the machinery of contracts now clear, the next step is to explore how these promises extend into the public arena—your sales and marketing. Because the moment you advertise, you make promises to the world. And in law, promises, once made, can bind you just as tightly as a signature.

Chapter 3 — Sales and Marketing Compliance

In business, few areas burn faster than marketing when mishandled. A single exaggerated claim, an unmarked endorsement, or a buried renewal clause can destroy the trust you've spent years building—and in the eyes of regulators, ignorance offers no defense. Marketing law is not about silencing creativity; it's about anchoring persuasion to truth. The goal is not to make your message dull but to make it durable, something that can survive both scrutiny and success. Entrepreneurs often move fast, testing offers and campaigns before reading the fine print, yet the law treats every public statement as a promise. Each ad, caption, or email carries weight. Understanding what "compliance" means in marketing is less about bureaucracy and more about credibility—the invisible currency that sustains every brand.

At the heart of compliant marketing is a simple principle: **truth in advertising**. It sounds moral, but it's actually economic. The marketplace depends on honest competition. Regulators like the U.S. Federal Trade Commission (FTC), the UK's Advertising Standards Authority, and the EU's Consumer Protection Cooperation network all echo the same rule—your claims must be truthful, evidence-based, and not misleading in context. "Not misleading" is the tricky part. The law doesn't only punish outright lies; it punishes implications that could deceive a reasonable consumer. If your ad says "clinically proven," you'd better have real, peer-reviewed data, not a handful of testimonials. If you say "eco-friendly," you need proof that your product's full life cycle meets that standard. The test isn't what you meant—it's what an average reader would think you meant.

That leads to the second cornerstone: **claim substantiation**. Every factual assertion—"reduces wrinkles in two weeks," "triples productivity," "saves 30% energy"—requires a factual backbone. The standard is "competent and reliable evidence." For health or performance claims, this often means scientific studies; for efficiency or cost claims, it might mean controlled trials or audited comparisons. Marketers often assume disclaimers can save them, but "results may vary" doesn't erase an unsupported statement. Substantiation must exist *before* you publish, not afterward when someone challenges you. The discipline of documentation—keeping records of tests, customer data, or research—turns creative risk into strategic strength. It allows you to speak boldly and defend confidently.

Promotions and discounts bring their own traps. A sale must be a sale in reality, not a psychological trick. Advertising a "50% off" discount on a price that never existed is considered deceptive almost everywhere. So is inflating a "regular price" to make a discount appear larger. The principle is consistency: the price comparison must reflect genuine history or normal practice. Even small businesses fall foul of this rule by copying the style of big brands without understanding their compliance infrastructure. Similarly, limited-time offers must truly be limited; "permanent urgency" is oxymoronic and, in some jurisdictions, unlawful. Honest urgency sells better because it feels authentic.

Another critical area is **pricing clarity**. The modern consumer faces a jungle of hidden fees and automatic add-ons. Regulators have responded with "all-in" pricing requirements—what you display must represent the real cost, taxes and mandatory fees included. The fine print can no longer contradict the headline. The spirit here is transparency: let the buyer know what they'll actually pay, when, and for what. Subscription services and recurring billing models, so common in the digital economy, demand particular care. If you offer a "free trial" that automatically converts into a paid plan, that transition must be crystal clear. Failing to disclose automatic renewals is not only unethical but increasingly illegal. Laws in the U.S., UK, and EU now require clear consent before charging renewals and easy, visible cancellation options. The click-wrap must show honesty, not entrapment. A compliant subscription disclosure answers four questions before sign-up: what it costs, how often it renews, how to cancel, and what notice applies. Anything less invites complaints and chargebacks.

Even something as simple as an asterisk can become a weapon. Footnotes and disclaimers should clarify, not contradict. When the fine print nullifies the headline, it's misleading by design. A solid rule of thumb: if you'd be embarrassed to read the ad aloud to your mother without the footnote, rewrite it.

E-mail and SMS outreach sit at the crossroads of marketing and privacy law. These channels remain powerful, but their abuse has turned compliance into a minefield. The governing principle is consent—explicit, informed, and revocable. In the U.S., the CAN-SPAM Act requires clear identification of the sender, truthful subject lines, and an easy opt-out. In the EU, the GDPR and ePrivacy Directive go further, demanding prior opt-in consent for marketing messages. SMS laws add another layer: because texts feel personal, regulators treat them as more intrusive, with fines rising per message. The rule is simple—if someone didn't ask for it, don't send it. Use double opt-in where possible, record timestamps of consent, and honor unsubscribes promptly. Violating these standards doesn't just risk fines; it erodes the one asset money can't buy—trust.

Social media has introduced a newer, subtler battlefield: **endorsements and influencer marketing**. A recommendation from a creator feels authentic precisely because it looks unscripted. Regulators know this and require transparency. If someone receives money, products, discounts, or any benefit for promoting a brand, that relationship must be disclosed clearly. "#ad" or "Sponsored by…" isn't optional—it's mandatory. Disclosures must be *obvious* and *proximate* to the endorsement, not buried in a sea of hashtags or placed after the "more" cut. The test is whether an ordinary viewer would understand the commercial connection immediately. Ambiguity equals deception. Brands are responsible, too; they can't hide behind their influencers' mistakes. Creating simple briefing guidelines—what to disclose, how to format posts, what claims to avoid—protects both sides. The smartest campaigns integrate honesty as part of the aesthetic; transparency becomes part of the brand voice rather than an afterthought.

Influencer compliance also extends to authenticity of claims. If a creator says, "I lost ten pounds using this product," it must be true *for them*, and their experience must reflect typical results or include a disclaimer that it doesn't. Fabricated testimonials or edited before-and-after photos can trigger legal action. What was once "marketing fluff" is now evidence in court. The digital record never forgets.

Another overlooked aspect of compliance is the **endorsement by omission**—failing to disclose a relationship can mislead just as much as lying about one. When a founder reviews their own product under a pseudonym, or when employees post glowing feedback without disclosure, it becomes astroturfing, a serious regulatory violation. Transparency isn't just an ethical choice; it's a strategic one. Consumers have developed a sharp instinct for authenticity. Brands that treat honesty as part of their marketing DNA build resilience that no paid campaign can match.

Promotional contests, giveaways, and sweepstakes introduce another layer of regulation, often varying by country or even state. "No purchase necessary" means exactly that; if entry requires payment, it becomes a lottery, and lotteries are tightly regulated or prohibited. Terms and conditions must specify eligibility, deadlines, and prize delivery details. Social platforms like Instagram and TikTok have their own disclosure requirements, too—ignoring them risks both suspension and scrutiny.

Beyond the regulatory landscape lies the ethical dimension of marketing compliance. It's tempting to view these rules as obstacles, but they actually serve as filters that force better creativity. Constraints sharpen clarity. A message that survives legal vetting often resonates more deeply because it's grounded in reality. Great marketers understand that credibility compounds. A brand that never deceives earns attention without shouting.

Sloppy renewals or hidden billing practices deserve special mention because they're both common and costly. Businesses sometimes bury renewal terms in dense contracts or rely on customer inertia. Regulators call this “negative option billing”—charging customers unless they actively decline. The backlash is growing. Consumers now expect frictionless cancellation, transparent pricing, and reminders before renewals. A simple email saying, “Your subscription renews next week—click here to manage it,” does more than satisfy law; it builds goodwill. Compliance here doubles as customer service.

The reputational harm from non-compliance often outweighs legal penalties. A public accusation of deceptive advertising, even if later disproven, can damage trust permanently. The internet remembers screenshots longer than court judgments. Compliance is preventive PR—it keeps your name off the wrong kind of headlines.

Ultimately, sales and marketing compliance isn’t about fear of fines. It’s about respect—for customers, competitors, and the truth itself. Every promise you make publicly binds you to a standard. The stronger your evidence and transparency, the freer you become to market boldly. You can push creative boundaries because your foundation is solid.

In practical terms, treat compliance as a collaboration between marketing, legal, and customer experience. Draft claims together, test promotions with internal review, and keep documentation of approvals. The process may feel slower at first, but it builds a culture of responsibility. Over time, it becomes muscle memory—a reflex to ask, “Can we prove this?” before you post.

As we move forward, we’ll explore the related frontier: how sales tactics and advertising intersect with privacy, consent, and digital tracking. The challenge now is not just to persuade, but to persuade ethically in a world where every click, like, and share is recorded. The businesses that master this will not only avoid penalties—they'll earn something rarer and more enduring: the trust of an audience that believes their word means what it says.

The theory of compliance means little until it's woven into daily operations. It's one thing to know the rules; it's another to make them live quietly inside your systems so they protect you without slowing you down. Most companies think of compliance as a legal department's burden—a stack of PDFs drafted once and forgotten. In truth, compliance is a living discipline. It's the connective tissue between marketing, product, sales, and customer experience. The more naturally it's built into your workflows, the less it feels like policing. A business that operationalizes compliance runs smoother because expectations are aligned from the first click to the last invoice.

The first foundation stone is a **clean and readable Terms of Service (ToS)**. For digital companies, it's the contract you sign with the world. Too often, ToS documents are legal swamps—copied templates dense with archaic language no one reads. But regulators now expect clarity, not obfuscation. Courts have ruled that hidden or unreadable terms can't bind consumers. The ToS should describe plainly what users can expect, what they owe, and how disputes are handled. Its job is twofold: protect your business and guide your customers. It should define service scope, data use, payment obligations, cancellation rights, and governing law, but written in human language. Simplicity isn't weakness—it's credibility. The clearer your ToS, the stronger your defense when challenged.

Within those terms, two sections deserve special attention: **refund and warranty policies**. These are the emotional flashpoints of commerce—the moments when trust is tested. A transparent refund policy turns disappointment into respect. When customers know upfront how and when they can request a refund, they're less likely to escalate problems publicly. Vague or buried policies create resentment and chargebacks. The same goes for warranties: define what you stand behind and for how long. In physical products, this means specifying coverage—defects, workmanship, replacements—along with exclusions. In digital services, it means being honest about uptime, data protection, and performance limits. You're not promising perfection; you're promising accountability.

Next comes **documented consent flows**, especially for digital products. Every modern company collects some kind of personal data, from emails to payment details to browsing behavior. Consent isn't a checkbox formality—it's a legal record of permission. You must be able to prove when, how, and for what purpose a user consented. This is the backbone of GDPR compliance in Europe, but even beyond that, it's a best practice. A clean consent flow uses clear language ("We'll email you updates about new offers. You can unsubscribe anytime.") and never bundles unrelated permissions. If you need consent for multiple purposes—marketing, analytics, cookies—each should stand on its own toggle. Store timestamped logs of every consent and withdrawal. In a world where privacy complaints can trigger multimillion-dollar fines, your audit trail is your armor.

Checkout disclosures are another point of vulnerability. Many businesses lose legal ground not through deception but through omission. When a customer completes a purchase, every material term must be visible before they pay: price, renewal terms, delivery timelines, refund rules, and any recurring charges. The "buy" button is legally significant; courts treat it as the moment of acceptance. If key details are missing or hidden behind multiple clicks, you risk claims of unfair or deceptive practice. The safest approach is radical transparency. Display total costs clearly, confirm order details in writing, and send a receipt that restates the essential terms. The goal is to make your customers feel informed, not trapped.

The **handling of customer complaints** is where theory meets emotion. Most disputes begin not in court but in inboxes. How your team responds determines whether they end there or escalate. Legally, responding promptly shows good faith; operationally, it protects your reputation. Build a documented process: log every complaint, categorize it (billing, product, delivery, privacy), and assign ownership. Set internal deadlines for response. Even if you can't resolve an issue immediately, acknowledging it and explaining next steps prevents frustration. For regulated sectors like finance or healthcare, complaint tracking isn't optional—it's required. But even in general commerce, it's a sign of maturity. Every complaint is free market research disguised as pain.

Compliance becomes sustainable only when it's shared. That means **coordination between legal, product, and customer success**. Marketing might create offers, but product teams build features that must match those promises, and customer success handles the fallout when expectations diverge. A compliant company is one where these teams talk early and often. If marketing wants to claim "lifetime access," product must confirm it's technically feasible. If product changes functionality, marketing must update descriptions. If customer success sees recurring confusion, legal must review the wording. The loop must be continuous. Many regulatory penalties stem not from malice but from misalignment—departments working in isolation.

Building **simple playbooks** transforms compliance from theory to habit. A playbook isn't a legal code; it's a guide your team actually reads. It should outline how to review marketing materials, approve new offers, respond to complaints, and manage data. It defines escalation thresholds—when something must go to legal and when it can be handled internally. This structure prevents paralysis because it empowers people to act confidently within guardrails. A junior marketer, for example, shouldn't need to guess whether a claim needs evidence; the playbook should say, "All performance claims must be supported by internal documentation or customer data." Such clarity replaces fear with discipline.

Technology can reinforce these habits. Automate what can be automated—store consent logs, flag missing disclosures, remind staff of renewal deadlines. Modern CRM and marketing automation platforms often have compliance modules; use them fully. But don't outsource judgment to software. Tools are mirrors, not brains. They help you execute, not decide. The human mindset behind compliance—honesty, consistency, documentation—remains irreplaceable.

When you operationalize compliance, you're not just protecting yourself; you're training your organization to think ethically. Every checkout page, every refund email, every complaint log becomes part of your brand's narrative. Over time, these systems create something money can't buy: trust at scale. Customers sense when a company plays fair. They respond with loyalty, referrals, and patience when mistakes happen. Regulation may compel compliance, but culture sustains it. The companies that endure treat compliance not as a cost center but as an operating advantage—a quiet strength woven into everything they do.

To see how these principles come alive, consider a scenario many modern entrepreneurs face: the **free trial funnel**. On paper, it's simple—a user signs up for a free month, enjoys the product, and either cancels or converts to a paid plan. In practice, this model has produced some of the most frequent legal headaches in digital commerce. The trouble starts when the line between "free" and "paid" blurs. Imagine a landing page boasting "30 days free—no commitment," followed by a checkout form that quietly collects credit card details and auto-enrolls users into a subscription after thirty days without explicit consent. That setup isn't clever marketing; it's deception.

A **compliant free trial** is transparent from the first click. The offer must state clearly whether payment information is required, what happens after the trial, and how to cancel. The transition to paid status must involve explicit consent—usually a checkbox or button labeled with unambiguous text like "Start my subscription after the trial." Automatic renewals must be disclosed in bold, not hidden in fine print. The cancellation process should be as easy as sign-up. Anything less risks violating automatic renewal laws, consumer protection statutes, or platform policies. Beyond legality, there's the reputational cost: users who feel tricked rarely return. A clean funnel, by contrast, builds confidence. It shows that you trust your product enough to let people leave easily.

Another concrete example involves **influencer partnerships**, which have become a core engine of modern marketing. Picture a fitness brand sending free supplements to a popular trainer in exchange for social media posts. The influencer posts a glowing review, but nowhere discloses that the products were gifted. Regulators treat that as a hidden advertisement—a deceptive practice. The fix is straightforward: disclose clearly and immediately. Hashtags like #ad or #sponsored must appear where viewers can see them before clicking "more." Vague wording like "Thanks to [brand] for the love" doesn't count. The key test is clarity. If an ordinary follower can't instantly tell there's a commercial connection, it fails.

Brands bear equal responsibility. You can't simply say, "The influencer didn't disclose properly." The law holds advertisers accountable for their agents' actions. Smart companies use influencer agreements that specify disclosure rules, review posts before publication, and keep copies for their records. This oversight isn't censorship—it's protection for everyone involved. When disclosures are honest and obvious, credibility rises. Consumers appreciate transparency, and campaigns perform better because trust compounds engagement.

Industry and regional variation adds complexity. A fashion brand selling globally must juggle European consumer directives, U.S. FTC guidelines, and Asia-Pacific ad codes—all similar in spirit but different in detail. For instance, a "14-day cooling-off period" for online purchases is mandatory in the EU but not in the U.S. A subscription disclosure that's compliant in California may violate stricter renewal laws in France. That's why local adaptation matters. A global template is a starting point, not a finish line. The more markets you reach, the more crucial it becomes to consult local counsel or at least stay informed through trade associations. Ignorance of jurisdictional nuance can erase years of goodwill overnight.

To simplify this complexity, every business launching a new campaign or product should follow a **pre-launch checklist**. Before publishing anything—an ad, a landing page, a collaboration—ask: Are all claims supported by evidence? Are prices and terms transparent? Is consent captured properly? Are influencers or affiliates briefed on disclosures? Has customer support been trained on refund and complaint procedures? This checklist is not red tape—it's insurance. It prevents problems before they become news. The best-run companies make pre-launch reviews routine, not exceptional.

Compliance also extends to subtle cultural expectations. A slogan acceptable in one country may offend in another; a humor campaign might unintentionally mislead when translated. Sensitivity is part of compliance. Regulators increasingly treat social responsibility as a legal expectation, especially in industries like health, finance, and environmental products. The future of compliance blends ethics with law.

As organizations grow, the challenge shifts from systems to people. Compliance cannot remain centralized forever; it must scale through culture. That means training new hires, empowering customer service teams to flag concerns, and rewarding honesty as much as creativity. The next phase of this journey—hiring and people practices—will explore how to extend legal and ethical discipline from products to the people who make and sell them. Because the same principle applies everywhere: integrity, once operationalized, becomes your most efficient form of protection.

Chapter 4 — Hiring and People Practices

The moment you bring another person into your business, everything changes. What was once a private endeavor now becomes a shared enterprise, bound by obligations you cannot outsource to instinct or goodwill. People decisions—who you hire, how you classify them, what you pay, and how you treat them—carry immense legal weight. Employment law, at its core, exists to balance power in the workplace, and misunderstanding that balance is one of the most common and costly mistakes entrepreneurs make. The irony is that most founders don't set out to break the rules; they simply underestimate how early those rules start applying. Even the first assistant, the first freelancer, or the first unpaid "helper" transforms your business from an idea into a regulated employer.

The starting point is classification: **employee versus independent contractor**. It sounds technical, but it defines everything—from tax liability to benefits, from control to risk. Many startups, eager to stay lean, treat early contributors as "contractors" without realizing that the label doesn't decide the reality. The law looks past the title on the invoice and examines the relationship itself. Across jurisdictions, the central question is always control: who decides what, when, and how the work is done? If you dictate hours, methods, and outputs, the person is likely an employee, regardless of what the contract says. True contractors operate independently—they control their schedules, tools, and workflows, and they typically serve multiple clients.

Different countries apply different tests, but the logic repeats. The U.S., for instance, uses the **"economic realities test"** and the **"common law test,"** both focusing on independence and risk. The U.K. uses a "personal service and control" analysis, while the EU and Canada apply similar multi-factor criteria. No single factor decides the outcome, but the pattern does. Misclassifying someone as a contractor when they function as an employee can unleash a cascade of penalties: unpaid taxes, back wages, social contributions, overtime claims, and even retroactive benefits. Governments are cracking down hard because misclassification undermines labor protections and tax revenue alike. The fix is simple but requires discipline: define relationships honestly, document them clearly, and review them as roles evolve.

Equally critical is understanding the doctrine of **"at-will employment,"** which governs much of the American labor landscape but not most of the world. Under at-will rules, either the employer or employee may terminate the relationship at any time, for any lawful reason, without notice. It sounds liberating, and for small businesses it often is—but it also invites risk when misunderstood. "Any lawful reason" does not mean "any reason." Discrimination, retaliation, or breach of implied promises still create liability. At-will status does not shield an employer who fires someone after they report safety violations, request medical leave, or refuse to engage in illegal acts. Courts read fairness into the gaps. The safest approach is consistency: apply written policies, document performance issues, and avoid impulsive decisions. Even in at-will environments, professionalism in termination protects both dignity and defense.

Outside the United States, employment relationships tend to be more structured, often requiring notice periods, severance, or formal cause for dismissal. European and Latin American systems, for instance, emphasize worker protection over flexibility. But regardless of geography, one truth stands firm: employment is never a casual transaction. Every hire is a legal contract, even when unwritten. The clearer you are about terms—duties, pay, schedule, probation, termination—the less room there is for costly misunderstandings.

No discussion of people practices is complete without **anti-discrimination laws**, which represent the moral spine of employment regulation. Every jurisdiction forbids some form of unfair treatment based on personal characteristics—race, gender, religion, disability, age, sexual orientation, and increasingly, genetic information or political beliefs. These aren't just legal boxes to tick; they're cultural markers that define your company's ethics. A business that tolerates bias, even inadvertently, will suffer far beyond the courtroom. The reputational damage of discrimination claims—magnified by social media—can eclipse any financial penalty. Compliance here begins long before a complaint; it starts in hiring language, promotion criteria, and company culture. Job postings should describe skills, not stereotypes. Interviews should assess ability, not identity. Equal opportunity isn't an HR slogan—it's a survival strategy in a world that demands fairness as loudly as profit.

Documentation remains your quiet shield. Every stage of the employment relationship—recruiting, onboarding, evaluation, discipline, termination—should be recorded clearly and respectfully. Not because you expect trouble, but because memory is unreliable when emotions run high. Performance reviews, attendance logs, signed contracts, and policy acknowledgments all create a trail of good faith. If a dispute arises, these records become your evidence of fairness. Without them, even a justified decision can appear arbitrary. The companies that navigate conflict best are not those without mistakes, but those with proof they acted responsibly.

One of the most misunderstood—and litigated—areas of employment law concerns **wage and hour rules**. These laws define who is entitled to minimum wage, overtime pay, and breaks. Many entrepreneurs assume that paying a "salary" exempts them from overtime. It doesn't. Exemptions depend on job duties, not titles or pay type. In the U.S., for example, an "exempt" employee must perform executive, administrative, or professional duties and earn above a threshold. Everyone else is owed overtime—usually time and a half for hours beyond forty per week. Similar protections exist globally. Misclassifying someone as exempt when they're not can result in massive back pay obligations and penalties.

Wage law also governs timing and transparency. Pay periods must be regular, deductions authorized, and pay slips detailed. Unpaid internships are another trap. Unless they meet strict educational criteria, they're often illegal. The assumption that "experience" substitutes for pay can backfire spectacularly when regulators intervene. The principle is straightforward: if someone performs productive work for your business, they must be compensated fairly and promptly.

Record-keeping requirements are less glamorous but equally vital. Keep payroll records, timesheets, contracts, and tax filings for the legally required duration—often several years. Modern payroll systems automate much of this, but responsibility remains with the employer. Losing these records doesn't just hinder audits; it weakens your defense in any wage dispute. When documentation is missing, courts often assume the employee's account is true. Precision here is protection.

Small businesses often stumble not because they intend harm, but because they treat compliance as an afterthought. They hire quickly, promise informally, and assume loyalty will prevent conflict. It won't. Every founder eventually learns that friendship is not a legal category. When you pay people to perform work, you enter a regulated relationship with obligations defined by law, not sentiment. That realization, far from limiting you, actually frees you. Once your structure and documentation are sound, you can manage confidently, knowing your good intentions are matched by good records.

Misclassification and **poor documentation** sit at the root of most employment litigation. They're expensive precisely because they seem harmless at first. You might think you're being generous by calling someone a "freelancer" to give them flexibility, but if they later file for unemployment or workers' compensation, the government may see it differently. You might think verbal agreements are enough with trusted staff, until someone's memory differs about a promised raise or bonus. Paperwork isn't bureaucracy—it's truth insurance.

Building compliance into hiring doesn't mean draining humanity from it. It means creating clarity so people can thrive. A transparent offer letter that explains classification, pay, benefits, and termination terms shows respect. A clear job description protects both sides: it sets expectations and provides criteria for fair evaluation. When onboarding includes policy acknowledgment—anti-harassment, confidentiality, device use—it prevents later surprise. Good documentation isn't just defense; it's design. It creates a culture of mutual understanding, where people know the boundaries and freedoms of their role.

Finally, remember that employment law evolves constantly. Minimum wage thresholds shift, discrimination categories expand, and remote work has redrawn boundaries across borders. The rise of the gig economy has blurred the line between autonomy and dependence. Staying compliant means staying curious. Review your classifications annually. Update contracts as roles change. Listen to employees—they often sense friction before lawyers do. Compliance here is less about perfection than vigilance.

Hiring people is one of the most defining acts of any business. Each hire represents both a leap of trust and a transfer of legal responsibility. The way you recruit, interview, and onboard sets the tone not only for your culture but for your compliance posture. A business can survive a bad product or a poor quarter, but a single mishandled hiring process—one that violates fairness laws, leaks confidential information, or creates contractual confusion—can leave scars that linger for years. A compliant hiring pipeline, therefore, isn't just about avoiding lawsuits; it's about designing a process where professionalism, transparency, and respect operate in sync.

The first step is **structure**. Unstructured interviews, full of improvised questions and subjective impressions, are breeding grounds for bias and inconsistency. Modern employment law increasingly expects objective, documented processes that demonstrate fairness. Structured interviews—where each candidate is asked the same core questions related to the job's essential functions—help prevent discriminatory patterns and ensure defensible decisions. They also make your evaluations sharper. When every candidate answers the same set of job-relevant questions, comparisons become about competence, not chemistry. Record brief notes after each interview. Should a rejected candidate later allege bias, your documentation will show consistent, skill-based reasoning.

Language in job postings and interviews carries hidden legal weight. Phrases like "young and energetic" or "digital native" might sound harmless, but they can be interpreted as age discrimination. Questions about family plans, health, or religion are almost universally prohibited. Instead of asking, "Do you have reliable childcare?" ask, "Our shifts run from eight to five—can you reliably meet that schedule?" The difference seems subtle but defines compliance. It's the difference between assessing ability and probing identity.

Once the right candidate emerges, the next compliance step is the **offer letter**. Many founders underestimate how critical this document is—it's the first binding agreement of employment. A clean offer letter summarizes title, start date, classification (employee or contractor), compensation, benefits eligibility, work schedule, reporting structure, and the at-will or fixed-term nature of employment. It should also contain two essential clauses: **intellectual property assignment** and **confidentiality**. These clauses protect your business's creative and proprietary assets from day one. The IP assignment ensures that any work produced in the scope of employment automatically belongs to the company, not the individual. Without it, ownership may legally stay with the creator, even if they were on your payroll.

Confidentiality clauses safeguard trade secrets and sensitive information—client lists, pricing, algorithms, and processes. They don't need to be intimidating; they just need to be clear. A mutual sense of respect and boundaries builds trust faster than slogans ever could.

Next comes the **handbook**, often dismissed as corporate fluff but in reality a compliance cornerstone. A well-written employee handbook is part guide, part shield. It sets behavioral expectations, explains policies on harassment, safety, attendance, time-off, and performance, and outlines procedures for complaints and discipline. Crucially, it disclaims that it is *not* a contract, preserving flexibility for both sides. Courts often view the handbook as evidence of company standards. A "sane" handbook, as some seasoned managers put it, avoids legal jargon and instead speaks plainly. Employees read it; managers reference it; lawyers respect it. It shouldn't drown in 200 pages of policy but should cover what truly governs daily life.

Once the employee starts, compliance shifts into training and documentation. **Required trainings** are the company's first defense against future misconduct claims. Anti-harassment and anti-discrimination training is now mandatory in many regions; others require safety or data privacy training. But even where optional, they're invaluable. They prove proactive intent—evidence that you took steps to prevent problems. Training shouldn't feel like a punishment or checkbox; it's a shared promise that everyone deserves safety and respect at work. Keep attendance logs and signed acknowledgments; regulators care as much about proof as performance.

Fair offers and required notices also extend into compensation practices. Transparency laws in states like California, Colorado, and several EU countries now require salary ranges in job postings. Wage theft laws require written notice of pay rates, payday frequency, and overtime eligibility. Even small omissions—a missing state notice or outdated poster—can invite fines. Treat compliance as communication: tell people clearly how they're paid, when they're paid, and what rights accompany that pay.

Every compliant hiring pipeline ends with a respectful exit strategy—a **termination playbook**. No one likes to think about endings during beginnings, but foresight prevents chaos. A proper termination process respects both law and dignity. Document performance issues long before they escalate. Provide written warnings when possible, outlining expectations for improvement. When termination becomes necessary, prepare a written summary citing objective reasons and referencing prior documentation. In at-will systems, you may not need a cause, but you should always have a rationale. Conduct the conversation privately, calmly, and briefly. Offer final pay promptly—many jurisdictions require payment on the last day. Collect company property, disable access respectfully, and confirm post-employment obligations like confidentiality or return of materials. A graceful exit is not just humane; it's strategic. Former employees can become future advocates or adversaries.

Modern businesses also face the challenge of **remote and multi-state teams**. The pandemic blurred the boundaries between office and home, and now geography no longer protects employers from local regulation. A remote employee in another state or country brings that jurisdiction's labor laws with them.

Minimum wage, leave entitlements, tax withholding, and benefits eligibility can differ dramatically. A company based in New York but employing someone in Oregon must comply with Oregon's sick leave rules. A European contractor might trigger GDPR obligations even if your headquarters is elsewhere. The simplest way to manage this complexity is to identify the "primary place of work" for each person and align policies accordingly.

For multi-state teams, payroll compliance becomes a technical puzzle. You may need separate tax registrations or local filings. Hiring through an Employer of Record (EOR) or Professional Employer Organization (PEO) can simplify cross-border compliance by handling local registration and payroll. But even then, responsibility for lawful treatment remains yours. Remote management also complicates confidentiality. Home networks, personal devices, and shared spaces increase data exposure risk. Extend your IT and privacy policies to remote workers explicitly, providing secure tools rather than expecting personal diligence.

Finally, integrate compliance into company culture rather than isolating it in HR files. Make fairness and documentation everyday habits. Encourage managers to take brief notes on significant discussions—praise as well as warnings. Standardize offer letter templates, onboarding checklists, and exit interviews. Consistency transforms compliance from reaction to rhythm. When everyone knows the process, you reduce not only risk but also anxiety. A compliant hiring system isn't mechanical; it's humane because it protects people from confusion and arbitrariness.

The most successful organizations view compliance as design, not defense. Each form, clause, and policy becomes an expression of your company's integrity. When the rules are clear and consistently applied, employees stop worrying about fairness and start focusing on contribution. The result is a team that trusts the system because the system itself is trustworthy. That is the ultimate function of a compliant hiring pipeline—not bureaucracy, but peace of mind.

Let's bring the principles to life through two common real-world moments that test even the most well-intentioned businesses: converting a contractor into an employee and handling a performance-based termination. Both reveal how compliance lives in the details—how documentation, timing, and communication turn potential risk into responsible action.

Imagine a growing design agency that started small, relying on freelancers for flexibility. One of those freelancers, Elena, has been with the company for eighteen months. She works exclusively for them, attends internal meetings, uses company software, and follows the same schedule as the full-time staff. What began as a contractor relationship has evolved, organically, into de facto employment. The founders realize that continuing to treat her as a contractor is risky: under labor law tests, she likely qualifies as an employee. Misclassification fines could reach tens of thousands, not to mention back taxes and lost benefits.

The transition begins not with panic but with transparency. The company reviews her role objectively—does she control her schedule? Does she bear independent risk? The answer is no. They decide to reclassify her properly. They draft a new employment offer, explaining pay structure, benefits eligibility, and tax withholding. The offer letter includes intellectual property assignment and confidentiality clauses that the old freelancer contract lacked. Because Elena contributed to key creative projects, they also sign a retrospective IP assignment, ensuring the company owns past work. This step, though tedious, closes a major legal gap.

Next, they notify their accountant and local tax authorities, registering her under payroll. They document the change internally: old contractor agreement terminated, new employment contract effective immediately. When Elena joins as a full-time employee, she receives a proper onboarding packet—handbook acknowledgment, policy reviews, and enrollment forms. The tone is collaborative, not corrective: “We’ve grown together, and now we want your role to reflect that.” Far from resenting the shift, she feels valued. Compliance, done right, strengthens relationships rather than straining them.

Contrast that with a company that ignores the issue. Months later, the tax office audits them, finds multiple “contractors” effectively working as employees, and demands back payments for payroll taxes, benefits, and penalties. The cost far outweighs what proper classification would have required. The lesson is clear: classification isn’t a label; it’s a factual condition. Regularly review how people actually work, not just what their contracts say. When in doubt, err on the side of formal employment—it’s safer, fairer, and ultimately cheaper.

The second example concerns a **performance-based termination**, perhaps the most emotionally charged event in management. Let’s say a sales manager, David, consistently misses targets despite coaching and clear goals. The company operates under at-will employment, but leadership wants to ensure fairness and avoid wrongful termination claims. They start by reviewing documentation. Over the past six months, David received two written warnings and participated in a performance improvement plan (PIP). Each meeting was summarized in writing, acknowledged by David's signature. The PIP outlined measurable benchmarks—conversion rates, client follow-ups, and timeline for review. It also offered resources for support: mentoring and updated training. Despite effort, results didn't improve.

When the decision is made, the HR manager prepares a termination summary referencing the PIP, prior feedback, and lack of improvement. The meeting is held privately with a witness present. The conversation is concise and respectful: "We appreciate your contributions, but the performance expectations we outlined have not been met. Today will be your final day." They provide final pay, information on benefits continuation, and collect company property. Afterwards, HR logs the documentation and sends a formal separation letter confirming the reason and referencing prior steps. The tone remains professional throughout—no personal critique, no surprises.

This process might seem elaborate, but it's what separates lawful, ethical termination from abrupt dismissal. If David later alleges unfair treatment, the company's records will show a transparent pattern of communication and opportunity to improve. Courts and regulators don't punish companies for terminating underperformance—they punish opacity and inconsistency. The same structure that protects the business also protects dignity.

As employment landscapes evolve, companies must track **limits and changing rules** that reshape what's permissible. Non-compete clauses, once standard in many industries, are now under intense scrutiny. Several jurisdictions have restricted or outright banned them, arguing they stifle worker mobility. Where still allowed, they must be narrowly tailored in duration and geography, and they must protect legitimate business interests, not suppress competition. Using a non-compete out of habit, rather than necessity, can render it unenforceable and even attract penalties.

Leave laws are another fast-moving frontier. What counts as paid sick leave, family leave, or bereavement leave varies not only by country but often by state or city. Remote teams compound the complexity: one company might have employees in four different regions, each with distinct leave entitlements. Failing to honor the strictest applicable standard exposes the company to penalties. A jurisdiction tracker—an internal document listing key labor obligations by location—can save enormous trouble. It needn't be sophisticated: a simple spreadsheet updated quarterly can keep HR aligned with current laws.

The deeper lesson behind these examples is that people compliance is dynamic, not static. Relationships evolve, laws shift, and intentions must adapt. Documentation, empathy, and curiosity are the only constants. A company that sees compliance as conversation—checking in, updating, explaining—stays agile. It treats law not as a burden but as a framework for fairness.

With your team in place—classified correctly, onboarded transparently, and managed with respect—the next step is to protect what that team creates. Every document, design, algorithm, or campaign they build is part of your collective intellectual capital. As Chapter Six will show, safeguarding those ideas is not only a legal matter but the continuation of everything we've built so far: clarity, ownership, and trust made visible on paper.

Chapter 5 — Protect Your Intellectual Property

Every business has something that makes it unique: a name, a product, a process, or a way of thinking that competitors can't easily replicate. That difference—your creativity turned into value—is intellectual property. Unlike physical assets, intellectual property doesn't wear out, doesn't depreciate with use, and can multiply without limit. One idea, well protected, can support an entire company for decades. Yet, surprisingly, many businesses guard it poorly or not at all. They focus on operations, sales, and growth, while their most valuable intangible assets—logos, designs, software, formulas, writings, or client data—remain unregistered, unassigned, and unmonitored. It's only when a competitor copies a product name or a former contractor launches a similar app that founders realize what they've lost. Intellectual property, once compromised, is rarely recovered intact. Protecting it is not just a legal exercise; it's strategy in its purest form.

The first step is understanding what counts as intellectual property and how each form operates. The law divides it into four main families: **trademarks**, **copyrights**, **patents**, and **trade secrets**. Each protects a different kind of creativity and carries different costs, durations, and enforcement methods. Knowing which applies to your business isn't about memorizing statutes; it's about recognizing where your value lives.

Trademarks are the face of your business—the words, symbols, and designs that identify your goods or services in the marketplace. A strong trademark distinguishes you from competitors and signals reliability to customers. Think of it as your business's DNA in commerce. Names like *Nike*, *Apple*, or *LEGO* are not protected because of their size, but because they are distinctive. In law, distinctiveness is the currency of trademarks. Generic or merely descriptive names—like "Best Cleaning Service" or "Tasty Burgers"—can't be registered because they describe rather than differentiate. The strongest marks are arbitrary or suggestive: they evoke meaning without explaining the product.

Trademark protection begins with use but solidifies with registration. In some countries, rights arise automatically from first use; in others, like much of Europe, registration is essential. A registered mark gives nationwide (and sometimes international) protection, allowing you to stop others from using confusingly similar names or logos. The process is relatively affordable but must be strategic. Before filing, always conduct a clearance search. It's heartbreaking—and expensive—to build a brand only to receive a cease-and-desist letter from a prior owner. Once registered, maintain the mark through consistent use and timely renewals. And remember: registration is only half the battle. Monitoring is the other half. If you fail to enforce your rights, they can weaken. A neglected trademark is like an untended fence—its borders fade until anyone can cross.

Copyrights protect expression, not ideas. They cover creative works—writing, music, artwork, photographs, software code, and even marketing materials. The rule is simple: the moment an original work is fixed in tangible form, it's protected. You don't need to register it for the right to exist, though registration strengthens your ability to enforce it in court. Copyright gives you exclusive rights to reproduce, distribute, and adapt the work. For authors and creators, this is the foundation of their livelihood.

In the business context, copyright issues often arise in two places: ownership and use. Many founders assume that if they pay for a design, video, or piece of code, they own it. Not necessarily. Under most laws, the creator retains copyright unless a written assignment transfers it. That means a freelance developer could legally reuse parts of your software, or a designer could claim rights to the logo you commissioned. The fix is simple but vital: every contract for creative work must include a clear IP assignment clause transferring all rights upon payment. Without it, you might only have a license to use, not ownership.

Conversely, when your team creates content—blog posts, graphics, training manuals—ensure they sign agreements confirming that all work produced in the course of employment belongs to the company. The term "work for hire" in the U.S. or "employee-created works" in Europe achieves this. Clarity on authorship prevents future disputes over who owns what, especially when founders part ways.

Copyright also protects your business from infringing others. Using unlicensed images, fonts, or music in your materials can lead to costly claims. The internet has made misuse effortless and detection even easier. Avoid shortcuts. Pay for proper licenses or use content explicitly labeled for commercial use. Fair use exceptions are narrow and often misunderstood; they don't cover convenience or ignorance.

Patents protect inventions—the functional, technical, and mechanical innovations that advance how things work. They cover processes, machines, compositions, or designs that are novel, useful, and non-obvious. Patents are the most complex and expensive form of IP, but they also offer the strongest shield: a time-limited monopoly, usually twenty years, during which you can exclude others from making or selling your invention. This exclusivity can define an industry. Pharmaceuticals, tech, and manufacturing firms rely on patents as their core defense. But for small companies, patenting requires discernment. Not every idea is worth patenting; some are better kept secret or protected through speed and branding.

The patent process demands disclosure—you must describe your invention in detail, enabling others to replicate it once the protection expires. That's the trade: exclusivity in exchange for public knowledge. If your advantage lies in secrecy rather than structure, you might be better served protecting it as a **trade secret** instead.

Trade secrets are the most underrated yet practical form of IP. They protect confidential business information that gives you a competitive edge: formulas, customer lists, algorithms, pricing models, manufacturing methods, or marketing strategies. To qualify as a trade secret, the information must have economic value from not being generally known, and you must take reasonable steps to keep it secret. That means confidentiality agreements, restricted access, password protection, and clear internal policies. Coca-Cola's formula is the textbook example—a century-old trade secret, never patented, never disclosed, and still central to its brand power.

The beauty of trade secret protection is that it lasts indefinitely—as long as secrecy is maintained. The danger is that once it leaks, it's gone. You can't reclaim a secret the world already knows. That's why robust confidentiality agreements with employees, contractors, and partners are non-negotiable. They don't just threaten penalties; they remind everyone of their duty to discretion. Trade secrets thrive on discipline, not locks.

Understanding these four pillars—trademarks, copyrights, patents, and trade secrets—gives you a map of your intellectual territory. The next question is where to start. Protecting everything at once is unrealistic, especially for small businesses. A **quick diagnostic** helps prioritize. Ask yourself: what aspect of my business, if copied tomorrow, would hurt most? If the answer is your name or logo, start with trademark registration. If it's your content, ensure copyright assignments and licenses are in place. If it's your invention, consult a patent attorney about novelty searches. If it's a process or customer database, strengthen confidentiality measures.

Think of IP protection like fortifying a castle. You don't build every wall simultaneously; you secure the gates that matter most. Over time, as revenue grows, you can layer protection. Many startups begin with trademarks and trade secrets, adding patents and international filings later. The key is momentum—don't delay protection until you "make it big." Success without safeguards only paints a bigger target on your back.

IP also demands maintenance. Registering is the beginning, not the end. Trademarks require renewals every few years; patents need periodic fees; copyrights depend on vigilance against infringement. Assign someone—internally or externally—to monitor deadlines and unauthorized uses. A simple spreadsheet tracking registrations, expirations, and enforcement actions can save thousands.

Beyond legality, protecting intellectual property shapes culture. It teaches your team that creativity has value, that innovation isn't accidental but deliberate. When employees understand that ideas are assets, they treat them with care. Contractors respect boundaries when they know ownership is clear. Investors take confidence when they see registrations and assignments in order. IP discipline signals maturity—it tells the world you intend to last.

In the end, intellectual property is not about hoarding ideas but cultivating them responsibly. It's the difference between being first and staying first. In every industry, imitation is inevitable, but competition need not be theft. When your brand, content, inventions, and know-how are legally fortified, you can innovate freely, negotiate confidently, and grow without fear that your own success will be used against you. The next sections will explore how to manage that protection in daily practice—how to document creation, share knowledge without exposure, and transform intangible genius into tangible security. Because in the modern economy, your mind is your factory, and the law is the fence that keeps it yours.

Knowing what intellectual property is only matters if you act on it. The gap between understanding and protection is where most businesses lose their edge. Every founder means to "get around to it," but trademarks are left unfiled, copyright assignments unsigned, and inventions publicly disclosed before patent deadlines. In the fast rhythm of building and launching, these omissions feel small—until a competitor seizes the opportunity.

Practical IP protection is about discipline, not paranoia. It's about turning ideas into recognized property before they become common knowledge.

The first and most urgent step for most businesses is to **file trademarks early**. Names and logos are the public face of your enterprise, and they're also the easiest for others to copy. Registering a domain name or Instagram handle does *not* give you legal rights to the name itself. Trademark registration does. The mistake many founders make is assuming they're safe because no one else nearby uses the same name. But trademarks don't operate by geography alone—they're organized by classes of goods and services, and conflict can arise even across borders or industries. Before investing in design, signage, or marketing, perform a clearance search through official databases or hire an attorney for a more comprehensive review. If the field is clear, file an application promptly. Early filing creates priority—your timestamp in legal history. Waiting, even a few months, can cost you ownership if someone else registers first.

Trademarks aren't only about names and logos. They can also protect slogans, sounds, packaging shapes, or even colors, if they uniquely identify your brand. The goal is distinctiveness. Generic or descriptive marks may pass unnoticed today but will crumble under challenge tomorrow. Think long-term. A good brand name balances creativity with registrability: short, memorable, and not already claimed. Legal reality should shape brand strategy, not follow it. Marketers and lawyers may seem like natural adversaries—one dreams, the other doubts—but when they collaborate early, you avoid the heartbreak of rebranding after success. A name with legal legs is worth more than one that merely sounds clever.

Once your brand identity is secure, turn to the heart of creative ownership: **copyright assignments**. This is where many companies, especially startups and creative agencies, stumble. The assumption that "we paid for it, therefore we own it" is wrong in almost every jurisdiction. Unless a written contract explicitly transfers copyright from the creator to the company, ownership remains with the author—be that a designer, developer, or freelancer. This misunderstanding has destroyed countless acquisitions when due diligence revealed that a contractor technically owned key assets. A proper assignment clause, signed at or before the start of work, avoids this catastrophe. It should state that all rights, title, and interest in any work created under the agreement belong to the company upon creation, with the creator waiving moral rights where legally possible.

For ongoing relationships, like recurring contractors or agencies, use a master agreement with a continuing assignment clause. Don't rely on verbal assurances or invoices. Courts enforce paperwork, not promises. If you acquire assets—like purchasing another company or hiring a team that built prior content—include IP transfer provisions in the transaction documents. Never assume ownership flows automatically. Paper it clearly.

Trade secrets demand a different approach. They can't be filed or registered; they must be *guarded.* Every secret is only as strong as the measures protecting it. A confidentiality agreement, or **NDA**, is your first line of defense. It doesn't create secrecy, but it defines it—what's confidential, how it can be used, and what happens if it leaks. For employees, integrate confidentiality clauses into offer letters and handbooks. For contractors and partners, sign NDAs before sharing sensitive data. Keep the language practical: specify that confidential information includes any non-public business, technical, or financial data, and that obligations survive after termination.

Beyond paperwork, protection means **access control**. Limit sensitive information to those who genuinely need it. Use password systems, secure servers, and clear digital hygiene. Label confidential files. When someone leaves the company, revoke access immediately and remind them of continuing obligations. Secrecy is not paranoia—it's professionalism. Trade secrets thrive in environments where confidentiality feels natural, not forced.

For innovators, **patent bars** are the silent deadline few founders know until it's too late. In many jurisdictions, once you publicly disclose or sell an invention, you lose the right to patent it. The U.S. offers a one-year grace period; Europe and most of the world do not. That means if you publish a paper, showcase your prototype, or launch your product without filing a provisional patent, you've forfeited exclusivity. Calendar this like a life-or-death deadline. A **provisional patent application** is a cost-effective placeholder that secures a filing date for one year while you refine or seek funding. If you decide to proceed, convert it to a full application before it expires. The calendar matters as much as the content—miss a deadline, and novelty is lost forever.

As businesses rely more on technology, the next compliance frontier lies in **open-source software and third-party IP**. Developers often use open-source libraries or code snippets to accelerate building. This practice is common and legitimate—but only if done knowingly. Some open-source licenses, like MIT or Apache, are permissive; they allow commercial use with attribution. Others, like GPL, require that any software incorporating that code also be released under the same license. That "copyleft" clause can unintentionally force you to make proprietary code public. For a startup seeking investors, that's poison. The cure is inventory. Keep a list of all external code, libraries, fonts, and assets used in your products. Know the license type, version, and obligations. Review them before release or funding rounds. The same principle applies to creative content—stock photos, fonts, or music clips. Just because it's online doesn't mean it's free.

Aligning product naming and brand strategy with legal reality completes the loop. Before every new product launch, run a miniature trademark audit. Check not only your name but also product lines, slogans, and logos. Make sure they're consistent with your registered marks and don't infringe others. Avoid naming products with variations of famous brands—parody is not protection. Also, be mindful of domain name disputes: cybersquatting regulations can punish opportunistic registrations that mimic established marks. Owning the domain doesn't guarantee trademark rights; the reverse is true—owning the trademark gives you leverage over domains.

Practical IP management isn't glamorous, but it's transformative. It turns creativity into capital and chaos into order. The companies that thrive are not those with the most ideas, but those that organize them into property before competitors do. A founder who understands this rhythm treats every creative act as a potential asset, every deadline as a defense, and every agreement as a shield. The law rewards that foresight with something rare in business: peace of mind.

Consider two familiar cautionary tales that illustrate the quiet power—and peril—of intellectual property missteps.

In the first, a young software startup hires an independent developer, Leo, to build the core of its platform. They agree verbally on payment and deliverables but never discuss ownership. The product launches successfully; investors express interest. During due diligence, the investors' lawyers ask for confirmation that the company owns all code. The founders realize that no assignment agreement exists. Legally, Leo still owns the source code he wrote. Under copyright law, payment for services doesn't transfer ownership unless a contract explicitly says so. The company has built its reputation, its valuation, and its roadmap on an asset it doesn't technically control.

When confronted, Leo isn't malicious, but he's cautious. He requests additional compensation for the assignment, arguing that the code's value has increased. The investors pause funding until the issue is resolved. Weeks of negotiation follow. Legal fees mount, timelines stretch, and confidence erodes. In the end, the founders pay more than they would have spent simply drafting a contract at the beginning. The lesson is searing but unforgettable: ownership doesn't arise from effort; it arises from evidence. A single signature could have avoided months of uncertainty.

Now imagine a different company—a boutique skincare brand launching its first line of organic products under the name "Pure Earth." The logo is elegant, the packaging complete, the marketing campaign set to roll. A week before launch, the founder receives a cease-and-desist letter from an existing company that registered "PureEarth Naturals" as a trademark three years earlier in the same product category. Their mark is federally registered and incontestable. The founder consults a lawyer, hoping to argue the difference in spacing or design. The lawyer delivers the hard truth: it's not enough. The marks are "confusingly similar," and continuing to use the name risks costly litigation. Overnight, the company must scrap packaging, rebuild the website, and rename its entire line. The rebranding costs nearly as much as the original production run. The founder feels robbed, but the real thief was delay. A simple trademark search months earlier would have revealed the conflict. Filing early would have locked in priority. Instead, the brand's debut became an expensive lesson in timing.

These two stories—one about code, the other about naming—show how intellectual property is not just a legal detail but the invisible architecture of trust. Investors, customers, and partners assume you own what you sell and can use the name you advertise. When that assumption breaks, everything built upon it wobbles.

There are also structural limits every business must recognize. The first is **cost**. IP protection isn't cheap. Trademark registration fees, patent filings, legal consultations, and enforcement actions add up quickly. But the cost of doing nothing is greater. Prioritize strategically: file what matters most, where it matters most. If your market is domestic, start locally; expand protection as revenue grows. Many businesses use a phased approach—register in key jurisdictions first, then in expansion markets once traction is proven. For startups, this staged strategy preserves capital without surrendering foresight.

The second limit is **timing**. Protection delayed often means protection denied. Patent applications depend on novelty, and public disclosure can destroy it. Even a conference presentation or crowdfunding page can count as public disclosure. Trademark filings operate on a first-to-file basis in most of the world, and copyright assignments lose clarity as memories fade. That's why maintaining an IP calendar is as vital as maintaining financial records. Set reminders for renewal dates, grace periods, and provisional deadlines. A missed renewal can erase years of protection overnight.

A third constraint is **public disclosure risk**. The modern urge to share—through social media, open demos, and investor decks—can unintentionally expose what should remain confidential. Once an idea becomes public, it can't be unshared. For patentable inventions, disclosure before filing destroys novelty in many countries. For trade secrets, it destroys secrecy altogether. The balance between marketing and confidentiality is delicate: show enough to attract interest, but not enough to enable imitation. When in doubt, file first, post later.

Managing all these moving pieces requires structure, not stress. An **IP inventory**—a living document listing all trademarks, copyrights, patents, trade secrets, and external assets—creates instant clarity. It helps you see what you own, what you license, and what needs action. Pair it with a **filing calendar** that tracks application status, renewal dates, and jurisdictions. Review both quarterly, just like financial statements. They're your company's creative balance sheet. Investors love seeing them because they signal competence and care.

Implementing these habits early pays exponential dividends. It prevents awkward surprises during due diligence, simplifies insurance coverage, and strengthens your negotiation power in partnerships. You can't license or sell what you don't clearly own, and you can't enforce what you can't prove. Good IP hygiene is the unseen infrastructure behind every confident negotiation.

Ultimately, intellectual property protection is an exercise in humility as much as ambition. It forces you to acknowledge that ideas, while born from inspiration, live in the real world of paperwork and procedure. The firms that endure are those that treat creativity as capital—worthy of accounting, maintenance, and defense.

With your brands registered, your code secured, and your inventions properly documented, you've built a moat around your business. Yet protection doesn't end with creation. Every modern company now carries another kind of asset—data. The next chapter turns to that invisible commodity, exploring how the information your products collect must be handled, stored, and shared. Because in today's economy, owning ideas is only half the battle; the other half is guarding the data those ideas generate.

Chapter 7 — Privacy and Data Basics

Modern business runs on data. Every click, purchase, message, and interaction generates it. For most organizations, data is not merely a byproduct—it's the raw material of growth. It shapes marketing strategies, improves products, and reveals customer behavior. Yet, the same data that fuels innovation also attracts scrutiny. Regulators, consumers, and courts now see personal data not as corporate property but as a form of identity—a reflection of human dignity that deserves protection. How you collect, store, and use it determines not only your compliance profile but your reputation. In the digital economy, privacy is no longer a matter of ethics alone; it's an operational necessity.

Understanding the legal architecture of privacy begins with recognizing **roles**—specifically, the distinction between *data controllers* and *data processors*. These two concepts define the entire framework of modern privacy law, from the European Union's General Data Protection Regulation (GDPR) to emerging U.S. state laws and global counterparts in Brazil, India, and beyond. The controller is the entity that decides *why* and *how* personal data is processed. The processor acts on behalf of the controller, following its instructions. Think of the controller as the architect and the processor as the builder. Both have duties, but of different kinds.

If your company determines the purpose of data collection—for example, deciding to store customer emails for marketing or to track website analytics—you are a controller. If you host or analyze data for another company under contract, you are a processor. Many businesses play both roles simultaneously: a software firm may process data for clients while also controlling its employees' and subscribers' data. The law recognizes this fluidity, but insists on clarity. Contracts must specify which party plays which role, outlining responsibilities, security measures, and breach notification timelines. When roles blur, accountability vanishes, and that's when violations multiply.

Equally important are the **lawful bases for processing** personal data. In older business models, collecting information was as simple as asking or inferring; now, every act of processing—whether collecting, storing, or analyzing—must rest on a lawful ground. The GDPR, which set the modern benchmark, lists six. The first is *consent*—freely given, specific, informed, and revocable. Consent works well for marketing communications or optional features, but it must be genuine. Pre-ticked boxes or vague statements buried in fine print don't count. The second basis is *contractual necessity*: processing required to fulfill a contract, such as delivering an order or processing payment. The third is *legal obligation*, where the law itself demands data retention—think of tax or employment records. The fourth is *vital interests*, used rarely, such as processing data to save someone's life in an emergency. The fifth is *public task*, relevant to authorities. The sixth, and most debated, is *legitimate interest*, which allows processing for business purposes provided it doesn't override individual rights. Each basis carries its own responsibilities and limits. Choosing the wrong one—or failing to identify any—creates invisible liability.

Outside Europe, the principles are converging even if terminology varies. The California Consumer Privacy Act (CCPA), the UK Data Protection Act, and frameworks in Canada and Singapore all echo the same theme: purpose limitation, minimalism, and accountability. Collect only what you need, use it only for the stated purpose, and secure it properly. The shift in philosophy is profound. Data law no longer treats personal information as a commodity to harvest; it treats it as a loan granted under trust.

Certain categories of information demand extra caution—what the law calls **sensitive data**. These include details about health, race, religion, sexual orientation, political opinions, genetics, biometrics, and in some regions, financial and geolocation data. Processing these requires stronger justification and often explicit consent. A fitness app tracking heart rate, for instance, must treat that information differently than a retail store managing email lists. Even seemingly benign data can become sensitive when combined. A customer's birth date, zip code, and purchase history, cross-referenced, can reveal identity with unsettling precision. This is why anonymization and pseudonymization—techniques that strip data of direct identifiers—have become vital compliance tools. They don't absolve responsibility, but they mitigate risk.

The foundation of privacy, however, isn't in forms or technology—it's in **transparency**. The most basic right of any individual is to know what's being done with their data. That's why every privacy regulation insists on clear, accessible privacy notices. A compliant privacy policy is not a wall of legalese hidden at the bottom of a website; it's an act of communication. It should explain what data is collected, why, how long it's kept, who it's shared with, and how individuals can exercise their rights—access, correction, deletion, and objection. The style matters as much as the substance. Regulators increasingly penalize opacity, not just misconduct. Writing plainly, updating regularly, and presenting information at the right time—such as pop-up notices when cookies are used or data is shared—build trust and meet legal standards simultaneously.

Transparency also governs **third-party sharing**. Every time you use analytics platforms, payment gateways, or cloud services, you extend your data ecosystem. The law expects you to vet those partners. Data processing agreements (DPAs) formalize these relationships, requiring processors to follow the same standards you do. It's not enough to assume they comply; you must ensure it contractually and, where feasible, technically. Controllers remain ultimately responsible for how their processors handle information. If a vendor leaks customer data, regulators will look at whether you performed due diligence before hiring them. Compliance, therefore, extends beyond your walls—it's a chain of accountability.

No privacy system stands alone without **security**. The two are twin pillars. You cannot claim to protect privacy if you fail to secure the data itself. Security obligations exist to prevent unauthorized access, alteration, or loss of personal information. Regulators expect "appropriate technical and organizational measures," which scale with the sensitivity and volume of data you hold. Encryption, regular updates, access logs, and incident response plans are no longer optional. A company that stores customer data unencrypted, or shares passwords via email, demonstrates negligence. But security is more than technology; it's culture. Employees must understand phishing risks, password hygiene, and data handling policies. Most breaches stem not from hackers but from human error—an email sent to the wrong recipient, a laptop left unlocked, a careless upload to a shared drive. Training is as crucial as firewalls.

When breaches occur, speed and transparency define the response. Most regulations impose **notification duties**—inform regulators within a fixed timeframe, often seventy-two hours, and affected individuals without undue delay if the risk is significant. Concealment multiplies penalties. The logic is simple: data subjects have the right to protect themselves. Companies that disclose quickly and take responsibility often recover faster than those that stall or deny.

One of the subtler challenges in modern privacy management is **data minimization**—collecting only what's necessary for a defined purpose. It runs counter to the instinct of analytics-driven businesses, where more data seems synonymous with more insight. But hoarding data you don't need turns from advantage to liability. Every record stored becomes another potential breach vector and compliance burden. Smart companies now design data flows around *purpose maps*: each dataset tied to a specific objective, reviewed periodically, and deleted when obsolete. Retention schedules, deletion protocols, and anonymization policies show regulators that you take responsibility seriously.

Privacy obligations also extend across borders. Global businesses must navigate data transfer rules—restrictions on sending personal data to countries lacking equivalent protection. Mechanisms like standard contractual clauses, binding corporate rules, or data protection agreements bridge these gaps. They're not paperwork for its own sake; they're legal bridges ensuring that privacy doesn't evaporate at customs. With the rise of remote work and cloud infrastructure, cross-border data flow has become unavoidable. Compliance now means designing systems that respect geography without constraining efficiency.

At the philosophical level, modern privacy law asks a question every business should answer honestly: if your customers could see exactly what you do with their data, would they still trust you? Transparency isn't just a regulation—it's a mirror. Those who embrace it win loyalty that no marketing campaign can buy. Those who hide behind complexity lose not only compliance but credibility.

The synthesis of these principles—clear roles, lawful bases, sensitivity awareness, and security discipline—creates a framework for sustainable data management. Privacy is not about saying "no" to data; it's about earning the right to use it responsibly. In the digital age, data is a privilege, not an entitlement. Companies that understand this shift—from ownership to stewardship—will thrive in both innovation and integrity.

As we continue, the next sections will move from principle to practice—how to operationalize compliance with privacy policies, consent mechanisms, and data handling procedures that survive audits and build trust. Because in the end, protecting privacy isn't about pleasing regulators; it's about keeping your promises to the people who made your business possible in the first place.

Turning privacy principles into daily practice is where most organizations stumble. Policies look impressive on paper, but compliance lives in the details—how data actually moves through your systems, who can see it, and what happens when things go wrong. Privacy cannot survive as an abstract virtue; it has to become operational muscle memory. Each company, whether a solo founder or a multinational platform, must translate lofty principles like "data minimization" and "accountability" into specific, repeatable behaviors that engineers, marketers, and customer service teams understand intuitively.

The first operational discipline is **data mapping**. You cannot protect what you do not know you have. Mapping data flows means tracing every piece of personal information from collection to deletion. Where does it come from? What systems store it? Who has access? Where is it sent? Most businesses discover, during this exercise, that their data ecosystem is far larger and messier than they imagined. Customer data hides in spreadsheets, backups, old email threads, cloud storage, and third-party tools. Marketing platforms collect analytics that no one reviews. Mapping brings this chaos into focus. It doesn't have to be perfect or technical at first—a simple inventory showing what data enters, what it's used for, and where it goes is enough to begin. From there, you can layer precision.

Once you know what you have, the next principle is **minimization**. Modern organizations collect far more information than they need, often out of curiosity or habit. But every unnecessary record is a future risk. Data minimization means gathering only what's essential for a defined purpose and deleting it when that purpose ends. It's a continuous discipline rather than a one-time purge. For example, a signup form asking for a user's date of birth when the service doesn't require age verification is a red flag. A CRM storing inactive leads from five years ago serves no legitimate purpose. Minimization also applies to internal access: not every employee needs visibility into every dataset. Role-based permissions enforce discipline quietly, ensuring that marketing can see campaign data but not payroll information, and engineers can debug without reading personal messages.

Transparency follows naturally. **Publishing clear notices** about how you handle data is both a legal and ethical requirement. These privacy notices should appear where collection happens, not buried behind a footer link. If you use cookies or tracking pixels, inform users before activation and give them control. If you send newsletters, include straightforward unsubscribe options. The purpose isn't to drown customers in information but to communicate honestly. The tone should be conversational, not defensive—"We use your data to improve your experience and never sell it without consent." A well-written notice builds confidence, signaling that your business respects boundaries rather than exploiting them.

For every external relationship involving data—vendors, cloud providers, affiliates—create **Data Processing Agreements (DPAs)**. These contracts codify how processors handle data on your behalf, ensuring that your privacy obligations extend downstream. A DPA typically defines the nature and purpose of processing, security standards, confidentiality duties, and breach notification procedures. Even small SaaS integrations deserve one, because regulators view the controller as ultimately responsible for its processors. A missing DPA is like leaving your front door unlocked and hoping the neighborhood is safe. Templates exist, but they must reflect your real operations. Signing one blindly without matching your actual data flow creates illusion, not compliance.

In today's interconnected world, few companies operate within a single jurisdiction. That makes **cross-border data transfers** an unavoidable challenge. Privacy laws restrict transferring personal data to countries without equivalent protections. The European Union, for instance, limits transfers to non-EU nations unless safeguards exist—such as Standard Contractual Clauses (SCCs), Binding Corporate Rules (BCRs), or adequacy decisions. The U.S. offers frameworks like the Data Privacy Framework to bridge this gap. Similar models are emerging globally. Handling transfers carefully means knowing where your servers and vendors are physically located and ensuring that proper agreements cover those movements. Transparency again plays a role—tell customers if their data may be processed abroad.

The foundation of both privacy and trust lies in **security**. Regulations rarely prescribe specific technologies because threats evolve constantly. Instead, they demand "reasonable" or "appropriate" measures. What's reasonable depends on the scale and sensitivity of your data. Encryption, firewalls, secure authentication, and regular patches are now baseline expectations. But security is not a product you buy; it's a habit you maintain. Train employees on password management, phishing awareness, and clean desk policies. Implement multi-factor authentication for all critical systems. Use anonymization or pseudonymization where possible. Regularly test your defenses through audits or simulated breaches. Remember: most data leaks stem not from malicious hackers but from preventable sloppiness—an exposed database, an unencrypted USB drive, a mistaken email attachment.

Preparation determines survival when incidents occur. A **data breach response plan** is not a formality; it's a playbook that can save your reputation. It should define what counts as a breach, who investigates, who communicates, and how fast. Many laws, including the GDPR, require notification to regulators within seventy-two hours of discovery. That deadline leaves no time for improvisation. Your plan should identify contact points for legal counsel, IT security, and public relations, along with templates for initial notifications. Conduct occasional drills, just as you would for fire safety. The goal is containment and candor—stop the damage, then tell the truth. Companies that respond decisively and transparently often emerge with more trust than before; those that hide or delay invite disaster.

Embedding **privacy by design** means integrating all these safeguards from the beginning of product and marketing development, rather than patching them afterward. When engineers build a new feature, they should ask: what data does this require, and can we achieve the goal with less? When marketers plan campaigns, they should verify consent sources and data sharing terms before launch. Privacy by design is not about saying no to innovation; it's about designing systems that protect users automatically. This mindset reduces future costs because retrofitting compliance is always more expensive than building it in. For startups, it's also a competitive edge: investors now routinely ask about privacy infrastructure during due diligence. A company that demonstrates privacy discipline signals maturity beyond its years.

Operationalizing privacy also means collaboration. Legal teams cannot manage it alone; they need cooperation from engineering, marketing, customer support, and leadership. Regular cross-functional meetings to review new tools, partnerships, or campaigns prevent blind spots. Appointing a data protection officer (DPO) or privacy lead, even informally, centralizes accountability. But the real shift happens culturally when everyone sees privacy as part of their job description. Just as safety became universal in manufacturing, privacy must become universal in digital business.

The operational side of privacy might seem procedural, but its moral core remains human: respect. Every record, form, and click represents a person who trusted you enough to share something. Protecting that trust is not about satisfying regulators—it's about keeping your word. Companies that operationalize privacy effectively find that it becomes not a drag but a differentiator. It makes customers more willing to share, employees more confident to innovate, and partners more eager to collaborate. Privacy, once treated as friction, becomes a foundation for growth.

Imagine a small but rapidly growing SaaS company, CloudLedger, offering accounting software for small businesses. CloudLedger stores customer data on servers operated by a third-party cloud provider and integrates analytics tools from several vendors. Under privacy law, CloudLedger is the **data controller** for its clients' user accounts—it determines why and how that data is processed. The cloud provider acts as a **data processor**, handling data on CloudLedger's instructions. To comply with regulations, CloudLedger drafts a Data Processing Agreement defining each party's obligations.

The DPA specifies that the processor must process data only as instructed, maintain security standards equivalent to CloudLedger's own, and promptly notify CloudLedger of any breach. It mandates encryption at rest and in transit, restricts subcontractors without approval, and sets timelines for deleting or returning data when the service ends. It also includes standard contractual clauses for international transfers since the servers sit in the United States and some clients are European. Both sides sign the DPA, store it in their compliance folder, and review it annually. This single document transforms what could have been a vague handshake into a verifiable compliance chain. When a client asks how CloudLedger ensures data protection, the company can point to specific contractual safeguards rather than vague assurances.

Later, CloudLedger faces a practical test. A European client exercises their right of access under GDPR, requesting all data the company holds about them. Because CloudLedger mapped its data flows early, it knows exactly where the client's data resides—application databases, billing records, and customer support emails. The support team routes the request to the privacy officer, who verifies the requester's identity and compiles the information within the statutory thirty-day window. The response includes both the data and an explanation of processing purposes, retention periods, and rights to correction or deletion. The client receives a complete, polite report, and praises the transparency. This small victory demonstrates how operational readiness converts regulation into trust.

A few months later, a real challenge emerges. An employee accidentally sends an export of several customer contact lists to the wrong recipient. The breach is contained within hours, but under GDPR, CloudLedger must assess whether the incident poses a risk to individuals' rights. The privacy officer consults the internal breach plan. The file contained names, emails, and phone numbers—sensitive enough to merit notification. Within seventy-two hours, CloudLedger informs the supervisory authority and affected customers, explaining the scope, the cause, and corrective actions taken. They reset passwords and reinforce email verification procedures. Because the company acted promptly and transparently, regulators acknowledge the response and take no enforcement action. The clients appreciate the honesty. The incident, while stressful, strengthens relationships instead of destroying them.

Contrast this with another company that ignored such preparation. When their system suffered a breach, they hesitated, fearing reputational harm. Weeks passed before disclosure. Regulators imposed heavy fines not because the breach occurred, but because of the delay and concealment. The comparison illustrates that compliance doesn't require perfection—it rewards integrity and readiness.

The landscape around these obligations is constantly shifting. Laws evolve with technology; what's compliant today may fall short tomorrow. The rise of artificial intelligence, biometric authentication, and data-driven advertising brings new layers of complexity. Some jurisdictions now require explicit consent for algorithmic profiling; others impose data localization requirements, demanding that personal data remain within national borders. A global company must monitor these changes continuously. The **roadmap** included with any responsible compliance strategy should track which triggers demand legal counsel: launching in a new country, implementing AI analytics, changing processors, or merging with another entity. Each event reshapes your data obligations.

Operational limits also arise from scale and cost. A startup cannot build the same privacy infrastructure as a multinational. What matters is proportionality. Regulators judge effort, documentation, and sincerity. They don't expect perfection from a ten-person company, but they do expect intent—clear notices, reasonable security, and responsiveness to individuals' rights. The myth that small businesses are "too small to matter" is dangerous. Breaches and complaints happen at every size, and public trust can vanish overnight regardless of company scale.

As privacy maturity grows, so does strategic opportunity. Clean data practices attract investors. During fundraising or acquisition, due diligence now includes privacy audits. Investors want assurance that customer data is collected lawfully, stored securely, and transferable under contract. A company with sloppy privacy habits may appear profitable but legally radioactive. CloudLedger's meticulous DPAs, access logs, and response records become proof of governance. When investors ask for compliance evidence, the founders provide structured documentation. This professionalism accelerates the deal instead of delaying it.

The broader point is that privacy management is no longer a legal afterthought; it's part of business hygiene. Just as accounting tracks money, data governance tracks trust. The two now intersect directly. Venture capital firms and acquirers view privacy compliance as a predictor of future risk. A business that mishandles data today might mishandle securities tomorrow. Conversely, a business that documents consent and disclosure can raise capital with confidence, knowing it won't trip over hidden liabilities.

Chapter 8 — Raise Capital Legally

For many entrepreneurs, raising capital feels like the natural next step after traction. The product works, customers are responding, and growth demands fuel. Yet, few realize that the moment you take money from anyone—whether it's a venture fund, an angel investor, or your cousin at the dinner table—you have entered the domain of securities law. This body of regulation exists not to slow you down but to ensure that investment, the lifeblood of enterprise, flows without deception or chaos. The rules are strict because history has shown what happens when they aren't. Every time you sell ownership in your company or issue debt that can be converted into ownership, you're offering a "security." And securities are never informal, even when the relationships are. The idea that "it's just between friends" has led countless founders into regulatory nightmares.

The foundation of legal fundraising lies in distinguishing between **accredited and non-accredited investors**. This distinction, codified in most jurisdictions but particularly central to U.S. securities law, defines who is presumed capable of bearing financial risk without extensive disclosure. An accredited investor is someone who meets certain financial thresholds—traditionally, a net worth exceeding one million dollars (excluding a primary residence) or an annual income above set limits for several years. The rationale isn't elitism but protection: accredited investors are considered sophisticated enough to assess risk without formal safeguards. Non-accredited investors, on the other hand, include nearly everyone else—friends, family, professionals, and early supporters whose enthusiasm might outpace their financial literacy.

The law allows you to raise money from both, but the pathway differs. Selling securities to accredited investors typically qualifies for **private offering exemptions** that simplify the process. These exemptions, such as Regulation D in the United States, allow companies to raise capital without registering a full public offering, provided they meet certain disclosure and advertising limitations. Within Regulation D, the most common route is **Rule 506(b)**, which allows you to raise unlimited funds from accredited investors and up to thirty-five non-accredited investors, as long as you provide sufficient information for the latter to make an informed decision. If you prefer to publicly advertise your offering, **Rule 506(c)** permits it, but then you must verify accreditation rigorously—collecting documentation rather than relying on self-certification.

Other countries offer parallel frameworks: the UK's Financial Services and Markets Act defines "sophisticated investors," Canada recognizes "eligible investors," and the European Union provides its own prospectus exemptions. The pattern is universal—private money can move freely when investors are presumed informed, but once you seek funds from the general public, disclosure becomes mandatory. Understanding where your campaign falls within that spectrum determines how heavy your compliance burden will be.

For small startups, **private offerings** are the most common route because they avoid the enormous expense of a public registration. Yet, even private offerings demand discipline. You must maintain accurate records of who invested, when, and under which exemption. Each investor should sign a subscription agreement acknowledging the risk and confirming their status. Failing to document these steps can haunt you later when you seek institutional funding or face an audit. Securities violations, even unintentional, can lead to rescission rights—meaning investors can demand their money back with interest.

Beyond the investor's classification lies the instrument of investment—the form that money takes when it enters your company. The main categories are **equity, notes, and SAFEs**.

Equity is straightforward: you sell shares in exchange for capital. Investors become part-owners, with rights that depend on the class of shares issued. Common shares usually go to founders and employees; preferred shares, often issued to investors, carry extra privileges such as liquidation preference or anti-dilution protection. Equity is powerful but irreversible. Once sold, ownership is diluted, and reclaiming it later requires buying it back or issuing more shares—both complex maneuvers.

Convertible notes are debt instruments that start as loans but can convert into equity under predefined conditions, typically during a future financing round. They allow startups to delay valuation negotiations until they have more traction. The investor lends money with the understanding that, instead of repayment, the amount will convert into shares later—often at a discount or with a valuation cap that rewards early risk. Notes have maturity dates and interest rates, giving them a legal character closer to debt than equity, even if their spirit leans toward investment. They are simple, flexible, and popular for early rounds, but they require careful drafting. A note that lingers too long without conversion can create repayment pressure or confusion over investor rights.

Then came the **SAFE**—the Simple Agreement for Future Equity—introduced by Y Combinator as a startup-friendly alternative to notes. SAFEs remove interest and maturity dates, functioning as a promise to issue equity when certain triggers occur, like the next funding round or acquisition. They simplify early-stage fundraising by removing the debt aspect, but they can also accumulate complexity when used repeatedly without conversion. Too many SAFEs can make capitalization tables unreadable, confusing both investors and founders later. Despite its name, a SAFE is not risk-free—it's a legal commitment that requires precise recordkeeping.

Each instrument serves a purpose, but all fall under the same legal umbrella: they are securities. Whether you issue shares, notes, or SAFEs, the underlying duty remains the same—to disclose honestly, document thoroughly, and comply with applicable exemptions. The form may differ, but the principle does not: investor protection through transparency.

As capital-raising platforms have democratized investment, a new pathway has emerged—**crowdfunding**. Unlike private offerings limited to accredited circles, equity crowdfunding allows everyday people to invest small amounts through regulated portals. Laws such as the U.S. Regulation Crowdfunding (Reg CF) or Europe's Crowdfunding Regulation create boundaries to balance opportunity with safety. Limits apply to how much individuals can invest based on income, and how much companies can raise annually. Disclosure is lighter than for public offerings but heavier than for private ones. You must provide financial statements, a business description, risk factors, and ongoing reports. The allure of community funding is real—it turns customers into investors—but it also exposes your brand to a broader regulatory lens. Once you accept money from the public, even in small increments, your accountability multiplies.

Crowdfunding works best when paired with realistic expectations. It's not free money; it's a compliance exercise wrapped in marketing. Running a successful campaign requires legal coordination, financial accuracy, and post-offering discipline. Regulators monitor portals closely because these offerings attract both novice investors and overzealous founders. Yet, when done properly, crowdfunding democratizes access to capital in ways once reserved for venture-backed startups. It fits the spirit of entrepreneurship while honoring the rule of law.

Regardless of method, the **recordkeeping** discipline that underpins fundraising cannot be overstated. Every signed agreement, investor questionnaire, proof of accreditation, and wire transfer confirmation should be stored systematically. These documents become the backbone of future due diligence. When larger investors or acquirers evaluate your company, they will examine your capitalization table line by line. Missing or inconsistent records can derail deals instantly. Investors want proof that shares were issued legally, that exemptions were valid, and that no undisclosed promises lurk in the shadows. Clean records are not clerical chores; they are trust made tangible.

Raising money legally also means respecting **advertising restrictions**. Private offerings, by definition, must remain private unless you qualify under exemptions that allow general solicitation. Posting investment opportunities on social media without verifying investor status can violate securities laws instantly. The line between sharing company milestones and soliciting investment can blur easily. A founder's excitement can become evidence of unlawful promotion if phrased carelessly. Always confirm what your exemption allows before you publicize fundraising plans. A lawyer's brief review costs far less than a regulatory investigation.

For international ventures, the complexity multiplies. Securities laws vary across borders, and compliance in one jurisdiction doesn't guarantee immunity in another. Offering shares to overseas investors can trigger foreign registration or disclosure duties. Global fundraising therefore requires localized strategy: consult counsel in each target country or limit offerings to investors who meet global standards of sophistication. The digital age tempts founders to think geography no longer matters, but regulators disagree. Jurisdiction follows the investor, not the server.

One consistent truth across all fundraising methods is that **trust and legality are the same currency**. The more transparent your process, the smoother your path to capital. Investors prefer clarity to perfection. They know startups carry risk; what they fear is uncertainty about whether that risk is lawful. A clean, well-documented raise tells them you take governance seriously. That seriousness compounds into valuation. Compliance, far from being a bureaucratic brake, often increases your company's perceived worth because it reduces hidden danger.

Entrepreneurs sometimes see legal structure as red tape rather than scaffolding, but securities law, like any other form of regulation, evolved from hard lessons. For every fraud or failed offering that shattered confidence, new safeguards arose to restore it. When you understand those safeguards, you stop fearing them. You realize they don't constrain ambition—they define it in durable form.

The essence of raising capital legally is respect: respect for investors, for the market, and for the truth. Each exemption, form, and filing embodies that respect in procedural language. When you comply, you're not appeasing regulators—you're proving you belong in a system built on trust. The next step after securing capital is learning how to manage it responsibly and stay within financial reporting standards. But before moving there, take comfort in this simple truth: legality in fundraising isn't about complexity; it's about clarity. A founder who treats every dollar raised as a covenant, not a shortcut, builds not only a business but a reputation that endures.

Raising capital is not only about convincing someone to invest; it's about proving that your company is ready to receive investment. Long before the first pitch deck leaves your inbox, the groundwork must be set with meticulous organization. Investors are not merely buying into your idea—they're buying into your records, your structure, and your discipline. The most successful raises are those that look clean before they even start.

That begins with the **capitalization table**, or cap table for short. It's the heartbeat of your company's financial structure. The cap table lists who owns what—founders, employees, investors, and option holders—broken down by share class, number of shares, and percentage ownership. A sloppy or outdated cap table signals disorganization and undermines confidence. A crisp one shows that you respect the arithmetic of ownership. Before raising a single dollar, review your cap table line by line. Verify that every issuance is documented, that vesting schedules are tracked, and that option pools reflect reality rather than aspiration. Nothing slows diligence faster than discrepancies between what founders think they own and what the records say.

Each change to ownership—new shares, SAFEs converting, or options granted—should be authorized through **board approval**. Even in small startups, the board (or the founders acting as the board) must formally approve securities issuances, usually through written consent. This isn't bureaucratic theater; it's a legal requirement. Failure to document approvals can invalidate transactions later or complicate mergers and acquisitions. Board resolutions should record the terms of the issuance, the exemption relied upon, and any authority delegated to officers. Keeping this paper trail from day one prevents the need for a costly cleanup when institutional investors arrive.

Next comes **discipline in communications**. In the enthusiasm of fundraising, founders often make statements that later haunt them. Promising guaranteed returns, sharing unverified financial projections, or casually posting about "investment opportunities" on social media can cross into securities solicitation. Even informal language—"we're opening a small round, DM me if interested"—can be interpreted as public offering activity. Under most private offering exemptions, public solicitation is strictly prohibited unless specific conditions are met. The rule of thumb is discretion: speak privately to prequalified investors, not publicly to the world. Emails, decks, and meetings should present facts, not forecasts you can't defend. Optimism is expected, but exaggeration is punishable.

When an investor expresses interest, the conversation formalizes through a **term sheet**—a non-binding summary of key deal terms. The term sheet sets the tone for negotiation and lays out the framework of the investment. It defines the valuation, amount raised, type of security (equity, convertible note, SAFE), investor rights, board composition, and closing conditions. Founders often panic at the sight of legal jargon, but term sheets are essentially checklists of priorities. Not every clause is worth fighting over. The key terms that define control and economics—valuation, liquidation preference, voting rights, and pro-rata participation—deserve attention. Others, like boilerplate legalese, can usually stand as is.

Understanding **information rights** is part of this maturity. Investors, especially institutional ones, expect access to company updates, financial statements, and major decisions. The law entitles shareholders to certain information by default, but term sheets often expand these rights contractually. Agreeing to provide quarterly reports or annual budgets is normal. What you must avoid is granting rights so broad that they slow decision-making or expose sensitive data unnecessarily. A fair balance gives investors confidence without turning every update into an audit. Transparency builds trust, but oversharing creates friction.

Closely related are **side letters**—separate agreements negotiated by specific investors, often granting special privileges beyond the main deal terms. A large investor might request early access to financial data, observer rights on the board, or favorable conversion terms. Side letters are legal and common, but they must be handled with caution. Each one creates a different set of obligations and, if undisclosed, can anger other investors later. Keep them minimal and consistent. If you must offer a side letter, ensure your counsel reviews its ripple effects across future rounds. What feels like a minor concession today could become a precedent tomorrow.

Equally crucial are the **filings** that accompany private offerings. In the U.S., most exempt offerings require a "Form D" filing with the Securities and Exchange Commission, along with corresponding state notices known as "blue sky" filings. These forms confirm your reliance on a specific exemption and provide regulators with basic information about the raise. Other countries have similar notice regimes. While these filings may appear perfunctory, neglecting them creates regulatory exposure that can delay or invalidate your exemption. Filing on time demonstrates that you take compliance seriously. It also prevents unnecessary scrutiny later when larger investors review your history.

Fundraising also demands awareness of what *not* to negotiate. Founders often waste energy arguing over details that rarely matter—attorney fee reimbursements, notice provisions, or document formatting. Focus instead on clauses that affect ownership and control. Learn when to hold firm and when to concede gracefully. Negotiation in fundraising is not about winning every point; it's about establishing a partnership. The investor across the table is not your adversary but your future stakeholder. The goal is alignment, not dominance.

If negotiation is about partnership, communication is about credibility. Every statement made during a raise can become part of due diligence later. Keep written records of correspondence, meeting notes, and any materials shared. Consistency across documents prevents accusations of misrepresentation. If you revise projections or metrics, label them clearly and explain changes. Founders who communicate openly through ups and downs often earn more investor loyalty than those who hide behind curated optimism.

Finally, remember that the end of the raise is not the end of your responsibility. After funds close, update your corporate records immediately: issue share certificates, record SAFEs or notes, and adjust the cap table. Deliver promised information rights promptly. Transparency is easiest when it's built into routine. A well-kept data room—a digital folder containing corporate documents, IP assignments, contracts, and financials—becomes your best friend during future rounds. Investors notice when everything is organized. Diligence-ready companies close faster and at better valuations because trust is already established.

Compliance and organization are not glamorous, but they are persuasive. Investors can forgive a young company for lacking revenue or polish, but they will hesitate if the paperwork looks chaotic. In fundraising, clarity is competence. When your records are clean, your communications precise, and your negotiations measured, you project the single quality every investor seeks before writing a check: reliability.

To see how these principles play out, imagine two realistic fundraising scenarios that capture the early stages of growth: a friends-and-family SAFE and a formal seed round. Both involve money, hope, and legal boundaries—but the tone, structure, and risk differ.

In the first case, a founder named Elisa is building a small tech platform. She needs $100,000 to finish development but isn't ready to assign a valuation. Her friends and relatives believe in her idea and want to help. She could simply take the funds informally, but that would risk violating securities law and jeopardize relationships if the project falters. Instead, she uses a **SAFE**—a Simple Agreement for Future Equity. The SAFE gives her supporters the right to receive shares later, once a proper valuation is set during a future equity round. No interest, no maturity date, just a promise that when professional investors arrive, their early support will convert into equity at a fair discount.

Elisa prepares a short explanatory note describing the risks in plain language: this is not a loan, there are no guarantees, and investors may lose everything. She limits participation to ten people, all of whom she knows personally. She avoids public promotion, relying on private conversations. Each investor signs the SAFE electronically and transfers funds directly to the company account, not to her personally. She keeps meticulous records—copies of agreements, a spreadsheet tracking contributions, and written board consent authorizing the issuance. After the round closes, she files the necessary regulatory notices under her jurisdiction's private offering exemption. It's small, but it's legal, transparent, and professional.

Contrast that with a **priced seed round**, where the stakes and scrutiny are higher. A year later, Elisa's platform gains traction. Angel investors approach, offering $1.5 million for a 20 percent stake. The deal involves negotiating a valuation, drafting a term sheet, and issuing preferred shares. The investors request standard protections: a one-times liquidation preference (meaning they recover their investment before common shareholders if the company sells), pro-rata rights to maintain their ownership in future rounds, and a board seat. Elisa reviews the terms with counsel, understanding which clauses matter most.

She accepts the valuation but negotiates board composition to maintain founder control. The round closes with properly executed share purchase agreements, updated corporate bylaws, and amended filings.

Both rounds succeed because Elisa respects the formalities. Her records are clean, her exemptions documented, and her communications restrained. She resists the temptation to post celebratory fundraising news online until all filings are complete. In doing so, she avoids the **advertising traps** that catch many founders unaware. Publicly celebrating an open raise can count as solicitation if not done under an exemption that permits it. The safer approach is to announce after closing, not before.

The **limits** of compliance emerge in subtle ways. For example, while federal exemptions like Regulation D govern broadly, individual U.S. states enforce **blue sky laws**—local securities regulations requiring notices and fees for each investor residing in their jurisdiction. Forgetting to file even one can create administrative headaches later. These rules vary widely, so maintaining a fundraising checklist—tracking investor locations, filing deadlines, and payments—ensures consistency. International investors introduce another layer: currency transfers, foreign ownership disclosures, and anti-money-laundering checks. Each layer demands attention, but none are insurmountable when approached systematically.

Advertising rules are another evolving frontier. The rise of online platforms has blurred the line between marketing and solicitation. Some founders use newsletters or podcasts to build awareness, inadvertently crossing into fundraising promotion. Even hinting that an investment opportunity exists, without proper verification of investors' accredited status, can void an exemption. The golden rule is intent: if your message could be interpreted as inviting investment from the public, stop and seek counsel. A single unapproved post can taint an entire round.

Compliance is not about fear but foresight. Most founders who run afoul of fundraising law never intended to deceive anyone—they simply didn't realize that securities rules applied to them. The remedy is preparation. A **closing timeline** ensures no detail slips: term sheet signed, board approval obtained, funds received in escrow, filings made within the statutory window, and updated records reflected in the cap table. After the close, deliver promised investor updates and maintain regular communication. The formality signals respect.

In both the SAFE and seed scenarios, one theme persists: **clean records win diligence**. When larger investors arrive later—venture funds, strategic partners, or acquirers—they will request every prior agreement, board resolution, and filing. If everything is organized, the process flows smoothly; if not, deals stall as lawyers reconstruct years of history. Good habits established early save immense time later.

Fundraising, at its best, combines vision with governance. You're not just selling ownership—you're selling credibility. Compliance, transparency, and organization demonstrate that your company deserves capital because it treats investors' trust as sacred. Each round, no matter how small, builds your reputation in a networked ecosystem where word travels fast. A founder known for meticulous honesty finds doors open more easily.

Once the funds are secured, the next challenge begins: protecting that capital and managing the risks that come with growth. Raising money legally is only half the journey; keeping it safe and resolving inevitable conflicts responsibly completes the circle. The next chapter turns to those protections—how to handle disputes, mitigate liability, and ensure that success isn't undone by the very risks it financed.

Chapter 9 — Manage Risk and Disputes

Every business, no matter how well intentioned, carries risk. Some of it is operational—missed deadlines, faulty systems, unreliable partners. Some of it is legal—breach of contract, employment disputes, regulatory violations. And some of it is cultural—the quiet erosion of accountability that allows small mistakes to fester until they become crises. Managing risk doesn't mean eliminating uncertainty; it means building systems that recognize and contain it before it explodes. Contrary to popular belief, compliance isn't about bureaucracy or punishment. It's about foresight—preventing problems so they never mature into conflicts. The strongest compliance programs aren't fear-driven; they're culture-driven. They give everyone in the organization the clarity and confidence to do the right thing without waiting for permission.

A good compliance program begins with simplicity. Many founders imagine that compliance requires armies of lawyers and thick binders of rules. In reality, it begins with a handful of clear **policies that matter**—living documents that explain how your company handles risk in practice. These policies cover how decisions are made, how information is documented, how money is handled, and how complaints are addressed. For a small organization, this may mean codifying only a few core policies: conflict of interest, data protection, anti-harassment, anti-bribery, and reporting procedures. Each policy acts as a map rather than a cage—it tells people where the boundaries are and whom to call when they're unsure.

Take a **conflict of interest policy**, for instance. It defines situations where personal relationships or financial interests might influence business judgment. The goal is not to prohibit relationships but to require disclosure. Sunlight, in governance, is the most effective disinfectant. Similarly, an **anti-bribery and gifts policy** clarifies what's acceptable when dealing with suppliers or clients. Small courtesies—meals, tokens, hospitality—may be harmless in isolation, but unchecked they can become systemic vulnerabilities. Having clear limits in writing allows employees to decline questionable offers gracefully by citing company rules rather than personal suspicion.

Next comes **recordkeeping**, the unsung hero of compliance. In law, memory fades but documents endure. Every policy, meeting, transaction, and approval should leave a paper—or digital—trail. The goal is not surveillance; it's continuity. Records prove that decisions were made thoughtfully and fairly. They also form your defense if regulators or courts ever ask for evidence. Good recordkeeping doesn't mean saving everything indiscriminately. It means identifying what's material and preserving it securely for the right duration. Contracts, financial statements, tax filings, employment records, and compliance certifications deserve long-term retention. Transient drafts, irrelevant emails, or duplicates can be deleted under a retention policy. Order replaces chaos when people know what to keep and for how long.

Modern recordkeeping also requires secure technology. Cloud storage and digital communication make access easy but increase exposure. Encryption, access controls, and audit logs turn documentation from vulnerability into strength. The most effective compliance systems treat digital hygiene as part of daily life: naming files consistently, storing them in centralized systems, and controlling editing rights. These habits sound mundane but often determine whether a company survives an audit intact or collapses under confusion.

Beyond internal order, **vendor oversight** represents one of the most overlooked elements of risk management. Every supplier, contractor, or service provider extends your legal footprint. When they fail, you may be held responsible by clients or regulators. Oversight begins with selection—choosing vendors not just for price or speed but for integrity and reliability. Conducting basic due diligence—checking references, reviewing financial stability, and confirming regulatory compliance—pays dividends later. Once engaged, vendors should operate under written agreements that define standards for confidentiality, data protection, safety, and performance. These contracts should include rights to audit, termination clauses for breach, and expectations around insurance coverage.

Oversight is not about micromanagement but accountability. A company that outsources payroll, marketing, or manufacturing cannot outsource responsibility. Regular reviews—quarterly or annual—confirm that vendors still meet expectations and comply with relevant regulations. This discipline is particularly vital in industries like finance, healthcare, or technology, where third parties may handle sensitive data. Many data breaches begin with a vendor's negligence. Having an oversight process—maintaining a register of vendors, verifying compliance certifications, and re-evaluating relationships—reduces exposure dramatically.

Perhaps the most transformative piece of any compliance program is **a culture of escalation**. In organizations where problems stay hidden, they metastasize. Employees often recognize red flags before management does, but fear, apathy, or confusion silences them. A culture of escalation changes that dynamic. It invites people to speak up early and assures them they won't be punished for doing so. The goal is not to encourage complaints for their own sake but to make problem-solving collective. A healthy culture teaches that identifying an issue is an act of loyalty, not betrayal.

Implementing this culture begins with leadership tone. Founders and executives must model transparency by admitting mistakes and welcoming questions. Formal channels, such as anonymous reporting systems or open-door policies, reinforce this behavior. When a concern arises—whether it's a suspected policy breach, financial irregularity, or ethical dilemma—the company should respond quickly and respectfully. Ignoring or trivializing reports is fatal. Each report, even if unfounded, is an opportunity to learn. The best organizations treat complaints as early warning systems. They analyze patterns over time, identifying recurring weak spots—an undertrained department, a lax process, a misaligned incentive—and address them before they trigger external crises.

Early issue spotting is not glamorous, but it's profoundly economical. Every legal dispute begins as a small, ignored signal: an unpaid invoice, a poorly written email, a disgruntled employee, an unclear clause. Catching these moments early saves more than money—it saves trust and reputation. A manager who notices inconsistent performance metrics can initiate a discussion before it becomes an accusation. An HR officer who receives an informal complaint can mediate before it turns formal. A compliance officer who detects irregular vendor billing can freeze payments before fraud escalates. These interventions require vigilance but not paranoia. They demand attentiveness grounded in process, not panic.

To make early spotting possible, companies must integrate compliance checks into their routine. Internal audits, regular reviews of contracts, and employee surveys are tools of prevention, not punishment. They reveal small fractures before they widen. The goal isn't to catch wrongdoing; it's to understand your own operations deeply enough that surprises are rare. Companies that conduct quarterly compliance check-ins—reviewing policies, risk registers, and key controls—develop an instinct for self-correction. Over time, that instinct becomes cultural muscle memory.

Technology can assist but not replace human judgment. Automated compliance dashboards, alerts, and analytics tools help monitor patterns, but someone must interpret the data and act on it. The best compliance systems combine automation with empathy. Numbers flag anomalies, but humans resolve them. When compliance becomes purely mechanical, employees stop thinking critically and start checking boxes. A balance between structure and sense keeps the system alive.

The irony of risk management is that it's most effective when it feels invisible. In well-run organizations, policies guide quietly in the background, like the operating system of a computer. You don't notice them because they work. They free teams to innovate without fear, knowing the boundaries are clear. That's what "prevent more than it polices" truly means—creating an environment where doing things right is easier than doing them wrong.

Small companies often believe they're too young for compliance infrastructure. Yet, the earlier it begins, the lighter it stays. Waiting until after a problem arises means retrofitting trust. A simple compliance program—just a few pages of clear policies, a shared document repository, a basic reporting system—can mature naturally as the business grows. What matters most is mindset: the belief that transparency and accountability are competitive advantages, not chores.

In disputes, documentation and culture decide outcomes as much as law. Judges and regulators respond favorably to companies that demonstrate good faith—those that can show they had systems, policies, and training in place. Even when mistakes occur, evidence of intent to comply often mitigates penalties. A company that self-reports a breach and cooperates will fare better than one that hides behind silence. The same holds true in civil disputes: a clean paper trail and reasonable conduct make settlement easier and litigation less painful.

Compliance is therefore not a department; it's an attitude—a way of running a business that values clarity over chaos. It transforms risk management from defense into design. When everyone in an organization knows the rules, feels safe to raise concerns, and trusts that leadership will act fairly, compliance becomes self-sustaining. Problems surface early, are resolved quickly, and rarely escalate into costly battles.

In the end, managing risk is not about fear of consequences but about respect for cause and effect. Every action leaves a trace;

every omission creates exposure. A well-designed compliance program connects those dots before someone else does. It keeps your business resilient, your reputation intact, and your focus where it belongs—on growth, not firefighting.

The next chapter will build on this foundation, showing how to handle conflicts when prevention isn't enough—how to resolve disputes strategically, preserve relationships when possible, and protect your interests when it's not. Because even the most disciplined companies eventually face confrontation, and how you manage those moments defines your true culture far more than any policy ever could.

Even the most careful business cannot eliminate every risk. Mistakes happen, suppliers fail, software crashes, and clients misinterpret promises. The purpose of risk management isn't perfection—it's resilience. The question isn't whether something will go wrong but how well you've prepared for the fallout. One of the most practical tools for this preparation is **insurance**, the transfer of specific risks to specialized institutions that can bear them better than you can. While policies are not magic shields, they can transform existential threats into manageable inconveniences when chosen and maintained correctly.

The first and broadest safeguard is **general liability insurance**, sometimes called commercial general liability (CGL). It covers bodily injury, property damage, and advertising injury caused by your business operations. This is the policy that responds when a customer slips in your office, when your delivery van dents another car, or when a competitor claims your marketing material defamed them. Even small businesses benefit from a basic policy because liability can arise from the most ordinary circumstances.

A single injury on your premises can lead to claims that outstrip years of profit. General liability coverage keeps these unpredictable hazards from destroying your balance sheet.

If your company manufactures, designs, or sells physical goods, **product liability insurance** becomes essential. It protects you when your product allegedly causes harm—through defect, improper labeling, or misleading instructions. The law often holds every participant in the supply chain accountable, from manufacturer to retailer. Even if you didn't cause the defect, you can be pulled into litigation simply because your brand appears on the box. Product liability insurance covers legal defense and settlements, making it indispensable for consumer goods companies, food producers, and hardware startups alike.

Service-based companies face a different threat: the cost of mistakes that don't injure people but still cause loss. That's where **Errors and Omissions insurance (E&O)**—also known as professional liability insurance—enters. It protects against claims that your services or advice caused financial damage. Consultants, accountants, designers, and software developers all rely on it. A coding error that shuts down a client's website, a marketing agency accused of mismanaging an ad budget, or a consultant blamed for poor strategic advice—all these fall under E&O. Without it, a single client dispute can become a company-ending event.

In the digital era, **cyber liability insurance** has become as important as physical coverage. Data breaches, ransomware attacks, and privacy violations can cripple operations and invite regulatory penalties. Cyber insurance helps cover forensic investigations, notification costs, legal defense, and even ransom payments under specific conditions. Policies vary widely, so reading exclusions is vital. Some cover only third-party claims, while others also reimburse direct costs like lost income during system downtime. Because the cyber threat landscape evolves constantly, this policy demands annual review to ensure it still matches your technology stack and risk profile.

For larger organizations, or any company with a formal board, **Directors and Officers insurance (D&O)** becomes crucial. It protects leadership against personal liability for decisions made on behalf of the company. Without D&O, a lawsuit claiming mismanagement, misrepresentation to investors, or breach of fiduciary duty could target executives individually. Even baseless allegations can require costly defense. D&O coverage gives qualified professionals confidence to serve as directors or officers, knowing their personal assets aren't at risk for good-faith decisions.

Finally, small businesses and startups often overlook **key person insurance**. This policy provides financial support if a founder, top salesperson, or critical engineer dies or becomes incapacitated. In early-stage companies, where success hinges on a few individuals, such a loss can halt operations. Key person insurance pays out to the company, not the individual's family, allowing it to recruit replacements or stabilize during transition. Investors often require this coverage because it secures continuity in leadership-dependent ventures.

Insurance, however, is only one layer of protection. Contracts and internal procedures define the others. Every significant business agreement should include a **dispute resolution clause**, drafted with foresight. These clauses determine where, how, and under what law disputes will be resolved. A well-written clause saves enormous time and money by preventing jurisdictional fights. If your business operates internationally, specify governing law and venue clearly—uncertainty benefits only lawyers. Many companies now favor arbitration or mediation clauses over direct litigation because they offer speed, confidentiality, and flexibility. Arbitration results in binding decisions enforceable like court judgments; mediation, by contrast, is collaborative and focuses on settlement. Choosing between them depends on the relationship's nature and the potential value of disputes.

Before invoking any formal mechanism, most conflicts begin with **a demand letter**—a structured communication outlining grievances, evidence, and proposed resolution. A good demand letter is both a negotiation and a signal. It shows the other side you're serious but willing to resolve matters without escalation. Courts often look favorably on parties who attempted to settle early. Writing an effective demand letter requires precision: avoid emotional language, state facts clearly, reference the contract or law, and define a reasonable timeline for response. Many disputes resolve at this stage because clarity replaces assumptions.

When prevention fails and litigation looms, preparation determines cost. Lawsuits are less about drama than about endurance and paperwork. The first step is **preserving evidence**. Once you anticipate litigation, you have a legal duty to preserve all relevant materials—emails, documents, notes, even chat messages. Deleting or altering them, intentionally or by negligence, can lead to sanctions far worse than losing the case itself. Implement a "litigation hold" immediately: freeze document destruction schedules and instruct employees not to delete communications related to the dispute. Modern discovery processes often involve terabytes of digital evidence, so early organization saves thousands in legal fees.

Budgeting for litigation is equally important. Many founders underestimate costs, imagining that justice follows truth rather than invoices. Legal defense involves filings, discovery, expert witnesses, depositions, and potential appeals. Even a straightforward case can drain tens of thousands of dollars. Establish a litigation reserve—funds set aside specifically for legal contingencies. Negotiate with your counsel on predictable fee arrangements where possible: flat fees for specific stages, capped hourly rates, or blended models. Transparency about cost expectations keeps stress manageable when conflict escalates.

Even during active disputes, negotiation remains possible. Mediation, often seen as an alternative to litigation, can also occur mid-lawsuit, saving time and preserving relationships. Unlike judges, mediators guide parties toward voluntary compromise. Their authority comes from trust, not force. Many jurisdictions now require mediation attempts before trial, recognizing that dialogue often achieves what judgment cannot: closure without bitterness. Settling doesn't mean surrender; it means choosing control over uncertainty.

Litigation, when unavoidable, should be approached strategically, not emotionally. Define objectives: are you seeking compensation, deterrence, or simply to protect reputation? Not every wrong deserves a lawsuit. Sometimes walking away costs less than winning. For disputes that must proceed, focus on evidence, not outrage. Judges respect documentation, timelines, and professionalism. Companies that maintain organized records and communicate calmly often prevail simply because they appear credible. The courtroom rewards preparation more than passion.

At its core, transferring and managing risk through insurance, contracts, and discipline reflects one truth: unpredictability is permanent, but vulnerability is optional. Businesses that acknowledge their limits—and insure against them—operate with confidence. Those that ignore risk gamble their future on luck. By blending financial instruments like insurance with behavioral safeguards like dispute clauses and early escalation processes, you create a safety net that allows ambition to flourish without recklessness.

Consider a mid-sized software company, BrightFlow, that sells workflow automation tools to enterprise clients. One morning, their largest customer claims the system crashed during a critical week, causing productivity losses. The client demands compensation equal to six months of fees and threatens to terminate the contract. BrightFlow's account manager panics and promises to "make things right" without consulting leadership. This impulsive statement, though well-meaning, could later be interpreted as an admission of liability.

Fortunately, BrightFlow's compliance culture includes a **clear escalation path** for potential disputes. The manager reports the issue to the internal risk team, which reviews the contract. They find that the service-level agreement (SLA) includes uptime guarantees but also defines remedies: service credits for downtime exceeding a threshold, not cash refunds. The team compiles evidence—server logs, maintenance notices, and correspondence—showing that the outage stemmed from the client's own firewall configuration, not BrightFlow's servers.

Before responding formally, the company drafts a **demand response letter**—polite but firm—explaining the findings and offering service credits as goodwill. They express empathy without admitting fault. The tone is calm, factual, and backed by documentation. This letter resets the conversation from confrontation to collaboration. The client, realizing the evidence isn't on their side, accepts the credits and renews for another year. BrightFlow avoids litigation entirely. The key was structure: escalation protocol, preserved records, and disciplined communication. No one improvised; everyone followed procedure.

In another case, a **security incident** tests the company's readiness differently. A phishing attack compromises several employee credentials, exposing some client contact data. Because BrightFlow has a documented incident response plan, the team reacts within minutes. IT isolates affected systems and notifies leadership. Legal counsel and the Data Protection Officer join immediately, triggering a predefined checklist. They assess the breach's scope, log all steps taken, and notify impacted clients within twenty-four hours. Since the compromised data was limited and encrypted, regulators determine that no formal enforcement is necessary. Clients commend the transparency. The same event, handled poorly, could have spiraled into regulatory fines and reputational ruin.

These examples underscore that risk management is not about avoiding bad days but surviving them intelligently. Every company will face moments of crisis; what separates the resilient from the reckless is preparation. BrightFlow's success lies in its consistent discipline: trained employees who know when to escalate, contracts that define remedies, and a crisis plan that transforms panic into protocol.

But even structured responses have **limits and tradeoffs**. One major pitfall is the misuse of **legal privilege**—the protection that shields communications with lawyers from disclosure. Privilege applies only when advice is sought for legal purposes, not business strategy. When teams blur those lines—cc'ing attorneys on every email or mixing counsel's advice with operational chatter—they risk waiving protection. Once privilege is lost, internal discussions can become evidence. The rule is precision: involve lawyers deliberately, not reflexively. Document facts separately from legal opinions. Counsel's value lies not in hiding information but in framing it properly.

Strategic tradeoffs also emerge in dispute resolution. Mediation may preserve relationships but yield smaller recoveries. Litigation can vindicate you publicly but drain resources. Arbitration offers confidentiality but limited appeal. Choosing the right path depends on long-term goals, not ego. Many companies fall into the trap of "winning" a lawsuit only to discover the victory cost more than settlement would have. Measured decision-making—guided by your risk appetite and cash reserves—is the essence of professionalism.

To institutionalize these lessons, companies maintain a **risk register**—a living document listing potential risks, their likelihood, impact, owner, and mitigation status. Each entry includes lessons learned from past events. After BrightFlow's phishing attack, for instance, the register adds a new item:

quarterly phishing simulations and multi-factor authentication audits. After the customer dispute, it adds contract review training for account managers. The register transforms anecdotes into systems. It turns experience into policy so mistakes are rarely repeated. Over time, the register evolves into a strategic map of vulnerabilities and responses—a practical counterpart to the compliance program described earlier.

A functioning risk management system is dynamic, not static. It grows with the company, learning from every challenge. What begins as a simple spreadsheet can evolve into integrated software tracking risk ownership, deadlines, and status updates. Regular reviews—quarterly or semiannual—keep awareness fresh. Leadership discusses the top five risks at each meeting, ensuring they remain visible. In this rhythm, risk management stops being reactive and becomes part of business planning itself.

Managing risk and resolving disputes ultimately test a company's maturity more than its luck. Problems reveal whether values and systems truly align. Businesses that communicate transparently, document decisions, and treat adversaries respectfully often emerge stronger from crises. The difference between chaos and composure is preparation, and preparation begins long before trouble arrives.

With risk and dispute management now integrated into daily operations, the organization moves from defense to sustainability. The next and final chapter will gather these disciplines—legal structure, governance, compliance, fundraising, and protection—into a forward-looking toolkit. It will show how to maintain this momentum, adapt to changing regulations, and scale responsibly without losing the discipline that made the foundation solid. Because in law and in business, endurance is the ultimate measure of success.

Conclusion: From Knowledge to Action

Every business journey begins with uncertainty. Founders often move through the early stages guided by instinct, energy, and improvisation, rarely pausing to consider the invisible framework that holds it all together. The legal landscape can seem intimidating—a labyrinth of contracts, filings, rules, and risks that threatens to slow innovation. But by now, after building this foundation step by step, you understand something essential: the law was never meant to cage creativity. When understood and used strategically, it does the opposite—it frees you to act boldly, knowing where the edges are. What once felt like a constraint becomes your scaffolding for sustainable growth.

This final chapter isn't about new rules or new documents. It's about perspective. The difference between businesses that survive and those that collapse often isn't intelligence, funding, or even product-market fit—it's foresight. Reactive companies panic at every setback because they've built nothing to absorb shock. Proactive companies, by contrast, anticipate friction and design around it. They use law as leverage, shaping their actions intentionally rather than scrambling to fix consequences. That shift—from reacting to predicting, from fearing rules to using them—marks the passage from beginner to professional.

Looking back over the journey, you can see how each piece of the puzzle fits together. You began by structuring your business properly, choosing the right entity to balance liability, taxation, and growth potential. That decision alone separated your personal life from the company's risks and gave investors and partners confidence in your professionalism. Then you learned the anatomy of contracts—how every clause, every signature, every definition serves to align expectations and prevent disputes. You discovered that agreements are not instruments of mistrust but of clarity, the written form of fairness.

From there, you turned outward to sales and marketing, translating legal obligations into customer trust. You learned that transparency in advertising, honesty in claims, and discipline in data handling are not bureaucratic burdens—they are the modern face of credibility. In an age when misinformation spreads faster than truth, compliance became not an obstacle but your differentiator. It told customers, "We respect you enough to be clear." And that respect, multiplied across thousands of interactions, built a brand no competitor can counterfeit.

When growth demanded capital, you learned how to raise it without crossing regulatory lines. You saw that fundraising, done cleanly, isn't a guessing game or an act of charm—it's a structured dialogue between preparation and trust. The clean cap table, the transparent term sheets, the correct filings—all those steps turned investors' caution into confidence. The clarity of your records became the silent proof of your integrity. For perhaps the first time, legality didn't feel like red tape; it felt like an advantage.

You also learned that protection doesn't end when money arrives. Intellectual property, data, and people form the living core of every modern business. Without legal care, those assets drift. With it, they compound. You built systems to safeguard your ideas through trademarks, copyrights, patents, and trade secrets. You learned to treat data not as a commodity but as a covenant between you and your customers—a relationship built on consent, security, and transparency. In doing so, you prepared your company for the next decade of business, where privacy and ethics will define brand loyalty more than advertising ever could.

Finally, you faced risk and conflict head-on, understanding that no company, no matter how ethical, is immune from mistakes or misunderstanding. The difference lies in readiness. You learned how to prevent disputes with simple compliance programs, to transfer unavoidable risk through insurance, and to resolve inevitable clashes through mediation, arbitration, or litigation with clarity and composure. You now know that conflict handled well can strengthen relationships instead of destroying them.

When these disciplines work together, something remarkable happens: fear gives way to fluency. You stop seeing the law as an unpredictable adversary and start using it as a fluent language. You can read contracts like stories, diagnose risks like patterns, and engage with lawyers as partners rather than translators. This fluency doesn't make you a lawyer—it makes you an informed leader. It gives you confidence to move faster, not slower, because your actions are grounded in structure.

To be proactive is to replace panic with pattern recognition. A proactive entrepreneur doesn't wait for a regulator's letter to care about compliance, or for a lawsuit to start documenting. They act early because they know early action is cheaper, calmer, and more credible. Proactive companies train their teams to escalate concerns without fear, review contracts before signing rather than after conflict, and treat recordkeeping as strategy, not chore. They measure success not just in profits but in predictability. That is what separates longevity from luck.

When law becomes leverage, it means you've learned to harness the same system others fear. You see that compliance isn't the enemy of creativity; it's its guardrail. You can negotiate fearlessly because you know what terms mean and what risks they carry. You can enter new markets because your structure and documentation already meet international standards. You can scale with confidence because your systems—contracts, policies, and governance—expand gracefully with size instead of collapsing under pressure.

This transformation doesn't require a large legal department or a bottomless budget. It begins with mindset. The businesses that thrive legally aren't those with the most resources but those with the most respect for precision. They document because they value clarity. They consult lawyers early not out of fear but to build speed later. They integrate compliance into product design, sales, hiring, and customer service, making it invisible yet omnipresent. When every part of your company knows how to think legally, you create a culture that prevents crises almost automatically.

That cultural shift—the internalization of law as everyday practice—is the quiet secret of resilient companies. It starts with leadership but spreads through habit. When founders model integrity, teams follow. When policies are written in human language rather than jargon, people read them. When escalation is encouraged instead of punished, problems surface early. Over time, law becomes part of how the organization breathes. Decisions are made with consideration rather than impulse, contracts are reviewed with curiosity rather than dread, and regulations are met with preparation instead of surprise.

From a distance, this maturity looks like calm. In reality, it's the product of discipline—an accumulation of small, thoughtful acts repeated until they form instinct. That instinct is your competitive advantage. In volatile markets, investors back the teams that look stable. Clients stay with the providers they trust. Employees give their best when they feel the company is fair and structured. Each of these outcomes is legal in nature, even if no one calls it that.

Law, in this sense, becomes a living architecture. It holds your promises, defines your boundaries, and protects your momentum. It tells partners and regulators alike that you play by the rules not because you must, but because you understand that doing so keeps the game worth playing. Entrepreneurs often speak of "scaling up." The truth is, you scale not by doing more but by doing right—consistently, transparently, and intelligently.

You've now seen how every dimension of your business connects to law. Entity choice anchors liability. Contracts define clarity. Marketing compliance protects reputation. Fundraising discipline attracts capital. Intellectual property secures innovation. Data governance earns trust. Risk management sustains resilience. Each of these topics is a gear in the same engine. Together, they create a business that can run not only fast, but far.

The journey ahead will still bring surprises. Regulations evolve, markets shift, and human judgment falters. But the foundation you've built is durable precisely because it's adaptable. The policies and principles in place today can be refined tomorrow; the key is to keep the habit of reflection alive. Review your systems periodically. Update contracts as relationships mature.

Train your team as laws change. Adaptation is not failure—it's proof that your company is alive and thinking.

The final message, then, is one of confidence. You no longer need to fear what you don't know. You've replaced guesswork with frameworks, chaos with systems, and anxiety with competence. The law will always evolve, but so will you. With the foundation in place, every future negotiation, partnership, or challenge becomes an opportunity to apply what you've learned.

You began this journey wanting protection; you end it holding power—the power to navigate complex decisions with composure. Where others hesitate, you can move decisively. Where others rely on luck, you rely on structure. The difference between the two is the difference between a gamble and a plan.

Law is not a bottleneck. It is leverage. It's the invisible architecture that turns vision into permanence. Businesses that master this truth don't just survive; they compound. They earn trust faster, recover from mistakes quicker, and grow stronger with every transaction. The principles you've absorbed here—clarity, documentation, foresight, fairness—will outlast trends, technologies, and markets. They are the foundations of enduring enterprises.

As you close this chapter, you don't need another checklist or form to fill. You need intention. Carry forward the mindset that has emerged: cautious but not timid, structured but not rigid, ambitious but responsible. Let the law work with you, not against you. Because when knowledge turns into action, and action turns into habit, you no longer just understand the law—you embody it in the way you lead. That is the real reward of this journey:

freedom through discipline, confidence through clarity, and the ability to build boldly on ground that will hold.

Translating knowledge into motion requires a plan. You've now absorbed the principles behind structure, contracts, compliance, fundraising, and risk—but information alone doesn't secure a business. Execution does. A 30-60-90 framework offers a rhythm: act immediately on what's essential, stabilize what's functional, and refine what's strategic. It transforms scattered tasks into momentum and keeps progress measurable. This plan isn't bureaucratic—it's pragmatic. The goal is to embed legality into the cadence of operations so it becomes habitual, not reactive.

The first thirty days focus on **formalizing structure**. By now, your entity should be registered, but structure is more than a filing certificate. Review your operating agreement or bylaws to ensure they reflect current ownership and decision-making reality. Many companies outgrow their original documents within the first year as partners join, roles shift, or new investors appear. Bring governance into alignment with how you actually operate. Confirm that ownership percentages on paper match the cap table, that voting rights are clearly defined, and that board authority—if you have one—is properly documented.

In the same period, address gaps in basic **corporate housekeeping**. Make sure all key resolutions, share issuances, and consents are recorded. Update your registered agent and confirm annual filings are current. If you're expanding internationally, map where subsidiaries or branches might be necessary for compliance or tax efficiency. The aim is not to multiply entities but to ensure every legal presence has a clear purpose and proper oversight. Order at the core prevents chaos at the edges.

By day sixty, shift attention to **contract standardization**. Most young companies accumulate agreements like driftwood—some drafted by lawyers, others copied from templates, many inconsistent. This is the moment to create harmony. Work with counsel to design a master set of templates: one for service agreements, one for NDAs, one for employment or contractor terms, one for vendor engagements. Uniformity saves time and minimizes risk. When every deal starts from a consistent foundation, negotiation becomes about business points, not missing clauses.

As you standardize, audit existing contracts for expiration dates, auto-renewal terms, and compliance obligations. Create a calendar or digital tracker so key deadlines never surprise you. This living database—your contract repository—should be accessible and searchable, not buried in emails. You'll thank yourself later during due diligence or audits when every agreement is one click away.

Parallel to contracts, **shore up people and intellectual property policies**. Ensure every employee and contractor has signed agreements covering confidentiality, IP assignment, and ethical conduct. Without these signatures, ownership of your core assets may remain ambiguous. Update your employee handbook to include anti-harassment, conflict of interest, and data-handling standards. These are not bureaucratic rituals—they're the framework of trust. For creative or technical teams, clarify who owns inventions and code. Make it explicit that all work created in the course of employment or contract belongs to the company.

This one sentence, properly documented, can save months of negotiation during acquisitions or funding.

As you approach day ninety, turn to **privacy and incident response**. Every organization, no matter its size, handles data—of customers, employees, or partners. Build a minimal but functional privacy framework. Draft a privacy notice in clear language, implement consent mechanisms, and establish procedures for access or deletion requests. Map data flows: where information enters, where it lives, who touches it, and where it exits. Once mapped, create a simple response plan for potential breaches. Assign roles before disaster strikes: who investigates, who communicates, who notifies authorities. Even a brief, rehearsed protocol can transform chaos into control.

During this period, conduct an **insurance review**. Bring all existing policies to one place—general liability, professional liability, cyber, D&O—and verify coverage levels and exclusions. Adjust as your business model evolves. A new product line, office, or client contract can shift your risk profile overnight. Schedule annual reviews with your broker so coverage keeps pace with growth. Insurance, when neglected, gives false confidence; when managed actively, it becomes the most cost-efficient hedge you'll ever buy.

Equally important is **cap table diligence**. As your company grows, each investment, option grant, or SAFE adds layers of complexity. Inaccurate cap tables are among the top reasons deals stall. Review all share issuances and confirm they match executed agreements and board approvals. Track vesting schedules and expiration dates. Keep your cap table digital and dynamic—tools exist to automate calculations, but accuracy still depends on human verification. A quarterly reconciliation ensures numbers stay credible. When the next investor appears, you'll be ready, not scrambling.

Before the ninety-day mark, **pre-brief your outside counsel**. Think of them not as emergency responders but as strategic partners. Send a concise overview of your structure, contracts, policies, and pending initiatives. Clarify who in your team can authorize them to act and what level of cost approval is required. Lawyers work best when they understand context early. Pre-briefing them with organized documents, checklists, and risk summaries allows faster, cheaper responses later. It's like onboarding a team member before the storm hits.

Finally, institutionalize **quarterly legal health reviews**. Every three months, gather leadership to evaluate compliance, contracts, and risk registers. Review what's changed—new hires, new vendors, new regulations. Ask one simple question: "If an investor, regulator, or journalist looked at us tomorrow, would we feel ready?" If the answer isn't an immediate yes, assign actions until it is. Over time, this cadence transforms compliance from a project into a rhythm.

A 30-60-90 plan doesn't end at ninety days; it creates habits that extend indefinitely. Formalize, standardize, strengthen, test, and review—that sequence repeats. The result is a company that grows confidently because its foundation stays solid while the world shifts around it. Legal readiness stops being a scramble and becomes part of your operating DNA.

Knowledge is only powerful when used. The systems you've built and the understanding you've gained will serve no one if they sit unused in folders or drive space. This final stage—the call to action—is where theory becomes advantage. It's the invitation to make legal readiness a daily reflex rather than a periodic chore.

Start by **adopting the templates** you've assembled or refined. Whether it's a standard service agreement, employment contract, NDA, or investor term sheet, consistency reduces friction. Every new deal should begin with a base document vetted for fairness and legality. It's far easier to adapt a solid foundation than to rewrite chaos each time. The goal isn't uniformity for its own sake but reliability—knowing that every new transaction begins from a position of clarity. When everyone in your company uses the same templates, negotiations shorten, misunderstandings shrink, and risk remains predictable.

Before signing anything new, make it second nature to **run a red-flag checklist**. This means pausing to scan for warning signs—clauses that shift liability unfairly, unclear deliverables, missing termination rights, or vague payment terms. The habit takes minutes but prevents months of regret. Checklists act as brakes on impulsive deals. They don't replace judgment; they sharpen it. A founder who learns to spot risk on sight protects their company long before lawyers ever read the document.

Escalate early when triggers appear. Most costly legal crises began as small doubts someone hesitated to voice. A suspicious clause, a sudden complaint, a rumor of non-compliance—raise it immediately. Early escalation isn't weakness; it's prudence. Encourage teams to bring concerns forward before they metastasize. Create a simple internal pathway—who to call, what to document, how to follow up. A two-minute conversation today can save hundreds of hours tomorrow.

Maintain a concise **"when to call a lawyer" list**. Not every question requires outside counsel, but some do. Call when signing major contracts outside your template library, negotiating large customer or vendor deals, issuing securities, responding to regulatory inquiries, receiving demand letters, or contemplating employee terminations that might spark conflict. Keep this list short, visible, and specific. It empowers your managers to act decisively without guesswork. Lawyers are not there to slow progress; they are there to protect it. The earlier they're involved, the cheaper and cleaner their advice.

Alongside these reactive measures, maintain a **living risk register**. This isn't paperwork—it's your radar. List ongoing and potential risks: regulatory shifts, supply chain vulnerabilities, data dependencies, pending disputes. Assign each a likelihood, impact, and owner. Review it quarterly, updating status and mitigation steps. The act of keeping it current keeps awareness alive. A company that reviews its risk register regularly rarely finds itself surprised. The register becomes a dialogue between leadership and reality, forcing honest assessment and disciplined response.

Growth, when sustained, depends on repeatability. A company that treats each legal event as a fresh crisis burns energy it could spend innovating. When readiness becomes a core capability, you scale without losing control. New offices, markets, and partnerships plug into established systems instead of improvising new ones. The same clarity that secured your first deal now multiplies across regions and teams. Legal readiness evolves from defense into offense—a source of speed and confidence.

Ethics remains the thread through it all. Every policy, contract, and checklist means little if used cynically. Compliance for appearance's sake breeds fatigue and mistrust. Real ethical discipline is quiet but visible in decisions: refusing shortcuts, correcting mistakes transparently, respecting data and people equally. In the long term, ethics and legality merge. The companies that endure don't ask, "Can we get away with this?" but "Will we be proud we did this?" That question, asked consistently, prevents 90 percent of legal problems before they start.

The end goal is independence—the ability to make legally sound decisions without paralysis. You won't need to memorize statutes or draft contracts from scratch; you'll know enough to ask the right questions and spot the blind spots. That self-awareness is your greatest asset. It allows you to engage lawyers, regulators, and investors as peers rather than dependents. You become fluent in the language of law, translating its abstract rules into practical advantage.

As your company grows, revisit everything you've built. Templates will need updates, policies will mature, risk registers will expand. Treat this evolution as proof of progress, not as maintenance fatigue. A living compliance system mirrors a living business—it changes because it's working. Schedule annual reviews not just to check boxes but to ask deeper questions: Are our values still aligned with our documents? Do our practices still reflect our promises? That reflection keeps legality human.

Ultimately, legal readiness isn't about paperwork—it's about freedom. Freedom to pursue opportunity without fear of collapse. Freedom to negotiate boldly, to partner globally, to innovate responsibly. When your foundation is solid, you can take bigger risks because they are calculated, not blind. Every entrepreneur seeks freedom, but only those who build structure achieve it. The paradox of law is that constraint, rightly understood, creates expansion.

So your call to action is simple: keep the engine running. Use the tools, refine them, teach them. Make red-flag reviews part of your onboarding, risk registers part of leadership meetings, and legal check-ins part of quarterly planning. Escalate early, document clearly, act ethically. With time, these habits become invisible, as natural as breathing. That's when you know you've crossed from compliance to competence.

This book began by promising leverage, and that promise now becomes real. Law is no longer the thing you fear—it's the framework that keeps your ambition upright. The checklists and systems you've built are not the end of innovation but its armor. You are equipped to grow confidently, ethically, and repeatably. You have transformed knowledge into discipline, and discipline into strength. From here on, every deal you close, every hire you make, every investor you welcome will rest on that strength. The next chapter is yours to write—not in contracts or policies, but in the story of a business that learned to lead with integrity, build with foresight, and move through complexity with clarity and grace.

www.ingramcontent.com/pod-product-compliance
Lightning Source LLC
LaVergne TN
LVHW022056200926
848481LV00003B/936